writing
with REason

writing with REAson

*The Emergence of Authorship
in Young Children*

Edited by

Nigel Hall

HEINEMANN

PORTSMOUTH, NEW HAMPSHIRE

Heinemann Educational Books, Inc.
70 Court Street   Portsmouth. NH 03801
Offices and agents throughout the world

ISBN 0-435-08498-4

© 1989 by Nigel Hall

First published 1989

First published by Hodder and Stoughton Educational, a division of Hodder
and Stoughton Ltd, Mill Road, Dunton Green, Sevenoaks, Kent.

Printed in Great Britain

Contents

About the editor

NIGEL HALL is Senior Lecturer in Education Studies at the School of Education, Manchester Polytechnic. He is a specialist in early developmental literacy and has written numerous articles on early literacy. He is also the author of *The Emergence of Literacy* (Hodder and Stoughton).

About the contributors

ROSE DUFFY is a classroom teacher and is currently undertaking an MEd at the School of Education at Manchester Polytechnic.

MARY GREAVES is a teacher at St Charles Primary School, Bolton. She is also undertaking an MEd at the School of Education, Manchester Polytechnic.

GEORGINA HERRING is currently a Project Officer for the National Writing Project. The data for her chapter was collected while she was a teacher at Chapel Street Primary School, Manchester. During that time she was a participating teacher in the Manchester section of the National Writing Project and was subsequently the Coordinator for the project based at the School of Education, Manchester Polytechnic.

LINDA JONES is a graduate of the School of Education, Manchester Polytechnic, with a special interest in early literacy. At the time her chapter was written she was a teacher at Norbury Hall School, Stockport.

SUSAN McCALDON is a teacher at Crowcroft Park Primary School, Manchester. She is a graduate of the School of Education, Manchester Polytechnic and has a special interest in early literacy.

JILL PAULING has taught in England and Germany, and is now teaching in a multicultural primary school in Hong Kong. Her research interest is in early writing development.

NANCY PEARSON is a second-grade teacher at Washington Elementary School, Moorhead, Minnesota. The project reported in her chapter was carried out with Althea Worth, a fourth-grade teacher in the same school.

JEANNE PRICE is a teacher at Beaver Road Infants School, Manchester. The project reported in Chapter 1 was carried out while she was a participating teacher in the Manchester section of the National Writing Project, based at Manchester Polytechnic.

ANNE ROBINSON is Senior Lecturer in Education Studies at the School of Education, Manchester Polytechnic. The material for her chapter was collected when she was spending a year as an infant teacher at St Chad's Primary School, Oldham. She is a specialist in early literacy development and the author of a number of papers on spelling and writing.

MIKE ROBINSON is the parent of Joseph Robinson. In any time left over he is a Lecturer in Geography at Manchester University.

VIVIENNE ROWCROFT is a teacher at Meanwood Primary School, Rochdale. The data for her chapter was collected while she was undertaking the Certificate in Educational Action Enquiry at the School of Education, Manchester Polytechnic. She has also served as the Coordinator for the Rochdale section of the National Writing Project.

JANETTE SHEARER is a teacher at Button Lane Infants School, Manchester. She is a graduate of the School of Education, Manchester Polytechnic, with a special interest in early literacy.

SUSAN WILLIAMS is a graduate of the School of Education, Manchester Polytechnic, and formerly a teacher at Benchill Primary School, Manchester.

Introduction

Nigel Hall

Most adults, if asked to say what an author is, would probably answer 'someone who writes books'. It is indeed true that authors do write books, and the publicity that such activities generate fixes in our minds images of what authors look like, how authors work, and what authors produce. People often hold such authors in awe – after all there has to be something special about anyone who can actually put together fifty, a hundred, or even two hundred thousand words. To achieve such a task usually requires education, a certain amount of intelligence, certainly perseverance, and some ability with language. In other words, authorship is usually seen as representing a high, and special, level of achievement and is most frequently associated with the appearance of a printed product.

That association is unfortunate because it leads to the denigration of efforts less successful than those of published authors; leads to limitations upon those things that can be considered as authored; and leads to the denial of authorship in beginning writers. It has the effect of restricting authorship to a kind of elite and makes access to membership of that elite extremely difficult.

Several hundred years' association with printed books has had a considerable impact upon our notions of what an authored text looks like. Has it influenced teachers when helping young children to develop as writers? Have we become obsessed with making our children's products look as perfect as a piece of published work? Have teachers, in their efforts to meet external demands for high standards of presentation, restricted children's experience of authorship? Have we separated becoming a writer from becoming an author to the extent that authorship has been devalued? Have we come to believe that young children cannot function as authors? Why do so many research reports and HMI surveys reveal young children doing little more than repetitious, low level skill exercises as the major part, and in many cases the totality, of their writing experiences.

Bennett, Desforges, Cockburn and Wilkinson (1984) offer a portrait of the writing experiences of children in the sixteen top infant classrooms that they studied. One such episode is recorded in some detail:

> The teacher talked to her class of 6-year-old children for 45 minutes about the countries of origin of the produce commonly found in fruit shops. This monologue was illustrated using a small map of the world and extensive reference was made to many foreign countries. She finished by asking the children to 'write me an exciting story about the fruit we eat'. The children had to decide what she meant by this! They were helped in part by the fact that they had heard this same instruction before in respect of other tasks. In fact the children wrote very little. They took great pains to copy the date from the board although the teacher did not ask them to do this. It was presumably taken for granted as part of the task specification. They formed their letters with great care and used rubbers copiously to correct any slips of presentation. Whilst this went on the teacher moved about the class commending 'neat work' and 'tidy work' and chiding children for 'dirty fingers' and 'messy work'. No further mention was made of 'exciting' content or of 'stories'. It seemed that the children knew perfectly well what the teacher meant when she asked for an 'exciting story about fruit' even though in this case the teacher's overt task definition, her instructions, stood in sharp contrast to the rewards she actually deployed.(p.6)

Even a low level analysis of this episode is sufficient to raise a number of issues relating to the teacher's views about the children's activities:

- She seems to assume that learning to write is about producing a first time correct, and neat, product. She thus forces the children either to write in those ways which they know by heart, or to queue for spellings. She also seems to think that the children need a model, (her talk) to guide them in what they write. Do they in consequence all write essentially the same things, resulting in cloned writing?

- She seems to assume the dominance of 'story'. It does not appear, at first sight, the obvious response to a 45-minute factual talk about fruit. She also seems to assume that the criterial quality of a story has to be that it is 'exciting', and that perhaps the only way children can be motivated to write is if it is 'exciting'. At the same time she appears to believe that the children cannot in fact write an 'exciting' story; she is happy to accept very little as a response.

- She apparently has the attitude that repetition or practice in similar tasks is the key to success in learning to write and seems to assume that allowing children to generate the content would be misplaced trust. Does she think it is beyond the capability of the children?

In giving them the content, concentrating on the visual appearance rather than the composition, requiring them to always write in the same style, accepting small amounts of writing as a response, and expecting them to make it perfect first time round, she organises it so that they have minimum possible responsibility for the composition of what they write, and maximum responsibility for the physical appearance of their work. Perhaps she believes that with plenty of practice in the 'appearance' skills the children will, one day, be able to take more responsibility for the content of their work, and then function more like authors. It is, of course, unwise to generalise from a single example. However the evidence of Bennett *et al.* would appear to indicate that this incident was, in fact, fairly typical of their observations in most of the classrooms in their sample.

In such situations there seems to be a clear separation between writing and authoring. It may not appear so to the teachers involved but, nevertheless, experiences of the kind related above restrict, almost totally, any opportunities for children to function as anything other than copiers, or practitioners of presentation skills.

The authors of this book believe very strongly that young children's experiences of writing do not need to be so negative, do not need to devalue the intellectual efforts involved in composing, and do not have to consist of endless routine practice. We believe that young children can function as authors.

What is authorship?

If we are to claim that young children can be authors we need to be clear about what we mean by the term 'authorship'.

The notion of authorship which underpins this book is that authorship is the reflective generation of written text. It is a belief that authors are people who make decisions; they take responsibility for the selection of what goes on the paper and are sensitive to the contexts in which they write, and to the audiences for whom they write. It is a notion that authors are people whose primary concern is with the meaning of what they write and are people who continually learn from the experiences of generating written texts. Authors, therefore, are people who use reason to write, and write with reason.

If the above definition is accepted, then it will be clear that a child who copies, or whose writing is firmly controlled by a teacher, cannot be an author, any more than an amanuensis, copy typist or random text generator is an author. The less responsibility a child has for his/her own text, the less the child can be considered as an author and the less the child can learn about being an author. A teacher who forces her children to copy or insists on taking control of the writing done by the children in her class can never know if the children can function as authors.

The definition of authorship used in this book has a number of implications for the way we view the written language potential of young children.

Authorship and decision making

Our notion of authorship implies that the intellectual processes which contribute to the development of a text are at least as important as the final text. Thus, to consider whether young children are authors, it becomes critical to examine the processes which accompany the generation of a text.

All authorship is complex because it demands making many decisions and orchestrating the results of those decisions into a coherent response. Authors have to make decisions about the context within which they are to write, the meanings they wish to express, the structure of the piece they are writing, and the representation of what they need to say. These decisions may be expressed in linguistic terminology as pragmatic, semantic, syntactic and grapho-phonemic decisions. Within any of these aspects, authors have to make decisions about how much freedom they have to maintain, explore, elaborate, reject, innovate and amend. All these decisions have to be welded into a coherent response in the production of a text.

To examine a young child's text by picking out only one aspect is to ignore the crucial orchestrated nature of the response. Thus, any analysis which focuses exclusively on a child's decisions about syntax, spelling or handwriting is a grossly inadequate analysis of young children's authorship. Equally, to examine a young child's text by concentrating on the product rather than the process is to run the risk of not knowing how, when, and what, authorial decisions were being made. This is not to say that the product is unimportant but, in helping young children develop as writers, attention to product should not be at the expense of attention to composition.

It may seem that some of the chapters in this book contain more about talk than writing. However, it is always talk about writing and it is this talk which has allowed us to follow authorship in progress, and which reveals so distinctly that children are intelligent decision makers about the texts they generate. It is this talk which enables us to identify young children as emergent authors rather than inadequate or incapable authors.

Authorship and intention

Our notion of authorship implies that a child's written product should be considered as a response to an intention to create a text for a particular context. A text may be syntactically simple but a highly appropriate, and very subtle, response to a particular need. It is therefore important to ask why a child worked in a certain way, rather than assume that the child should have worked in another way.

All the authors of this book believe that young children are reflective people and that they usually act with serious intent; in other words children have reasons for the things they do. We do not assume that because children are young they act randomly and without thought. Children may not always act in ways that make immediate sense to adults, but that rarely means an act is without sense. It is usually simply the limitations of experience which lead children to come to conclusions which are different to ours. This is as true of authoring as it is of all other aspects of life. When children generate texts we must, therefore, seek the intention behind text; we must try to identify the child's interpretation of the task, and his/her view about how that task should be tackled.

The chapters in this book offer convincing evidence of children's abilities to make judgments about the contexts for which they are writing, and to formulate intentions for what they are going to write. They show us children who can distinguish between writing for teachers as teachers and writing for teachers as people; children who can work out the social relationship between them and correspondents when they author letters; children who consider the reader when they compose their stories; and children who create texts with an understanding of the effect they will have on an audience.

Authorship and all texts

Our notion of authorship implies that any text, the composition of which demands intellectual judgments, must be considered to have been authored. Therefore, in looking for evidence about young children's authorship it becomes imperative to look for it amongst the production of the widest possible range of genres. It is impossible to know whether children are sensitive to demands of producing different types of texts unless one examines their performance in different contexts.

Once it is accepted that authorship is the reflective generation of texts, then the process of producing any text which demands thought must be authorship. Children spend far more time writing stories than they do on any other type of text, yet other types of genres often make interesting intellectual demands upon children. All texts are produced for particular contexts and these contexts have built into them certain demands. If a text is to be effective it must be a response to these demands.

In our everyday lives we meet a wide range of texts, many of which turn out to be very important to us. Advertising slogans seduce us; political slogans repel us; health messages frighten us; government forms collect information from us; bank statements horrify us; signs warn us; messages irritate us; lists remind us; labels help us; cartoons amuse us; crime stories puzzle us; signposts direct us; instructions guide us; birthday cards make us feel wanted; poems make us reflective; graffiti intrigues us; headlines grab us; old love letters make us nostalgic; newspapers keep us up to date; letters keep us in touch; and diaries keep us on time.

For all these situations someone has produced a text; not any old text but one which is best suited for its purpose. In order for this to happen it has had to be produced by someone capable of reflecting upon the needs of the context. It is easy to demean the kind of writing needed for many of these situations but, at the same time, it is often incredibly difficult to author a simple text that works. Anyone who doubts it should try coining a totally memorable advertising slogan, a book title, or a name for a new product.

Children grow up in a world where they are surrounded by a wide variety of authored texts. The world is full of demonstrations. A classroom environment which features these kinds of print and allows children to explore them, both as readers and writers, is one which facilitates the development of authorship.

There are relatively few chapters in this book about story writing; the majority of the chapters deal with other aspects of authorship. This is not because story writing is considered unimportant; indeed, it is crucial in offering children opportunities to create extended fictions and to perhaps handle some of their own experiences in reflective ways. However, this book does attempt to show that young children can be authors of many kinds of texts. Thus the chapters offer extended exploration of dialogue in letters and journals, rule making, message construction, reviews, as well as stories. In all the chapters children can be seen to be responsive to contextual constraints and readership constraints.

Authorship and growth

Our notion of authorship implies that all authors become more accomplished as a result of continuing experiences in making meanings with print. In other words, they learn from their authorship experiences.

Young children successfully learn concepts and ideas by having experiences with the things that those ideas and concepts represent. Thus, we should anticipate that given purposeful opportunities to make meanings with written language, they will make sense of authorship.

It is important to think of young children not as people who cannot be authors, but as people who have had little experience of being authors. Therefore, the range of background knowledge upon which they can draw is limited. The result of limited experience is, inevitably, a restricted range of responses to the demands of authorship. However, this does not in any way mean that children fail to function as authors. The chapters in this book show time and time again children who use, in appropriate ways, their limited experiences to formulate reasoned texts. The chapters also show children, time and time again, drawing upon print to help them sort out their ideas. Children read letters, search books, collect leaflets, and generally use print in the world as a source for their theories about authorship.

It should be remembered that young children are in exactly the same state as all of us who author texts. There is not, unfortunately, any point in life at which one can say 'I have conquered authorship'. Growth in authorship ends when people stop thinking about what they write; for many people that means authorship ends when life ends. Every time someone is faced with creating a text for a novel situation a whole set of decisions have to be faced. The greater the diversity of authoring experiences, the wider the repertoire upon which they can draw. It would be a grave error to equate the end of formal schooling with the achievement of literacy.

If it is experience of authorship which helps authors develop, then it follows that children should, from the start, be given opportunities to explore what it means to be an author. Thus the development of authorship should be continuous. Metamorphosis theories of authorship which assume that in order to become an author children have got to be something else first – a good handwriter, a good speller etc. – rely too much on hope. We know only too well that such hope frequently fails to be realised.

The following chapters demonstrate situations within which children were able to grow as authors. Children had space to think about what they were doing; they were able to grow as authors because the experiences were open-entried, and open-ended. They were also extremely enjoyable; they were fun. They were not turgid, dry, repetitious, boring, or negative. Being an author is hard work, and it goes on being hard, but it can still be enjoyable and immensely satisfying.

If the unaided written language behaviours of young children are examined while bearing in mind the above points, then a picture emerges of children who are functioning extremely rationally in the ways they make meanings. Their work may not always be neat, it may not be spelled correctly, and it may often be without punctuation but what can be seen is authorship in action; children who are, from the start, reflective generators of text.

That the focus in this book is on the compositional qualities of writing does not imply, in any way whatsoever, that the authors do not have concern that children become authors who can spell, punctuate, and write neatly. It means that they do not see those skills as ends in themselves but as contributions to the more effective realisation of authorship, and that as 'contributions' they take their place alongside the development of other authorial abilities and do not dominate or displace them.

Outline of the book

All except one of the following chapters have been written by people who were, at the time of doing the study, practising classroom teachers. All the work was carried out within their normal teaching commitment. The book does not attempt to offer a comprehensive coverage of young children's emerging authorship. Indeed, there are many aspects of authorship not covered in the following chapters – not because they are unimportant, but simply because they did not happen to be a focus of the investigations carried out by this group of teachers. The studies reported here are beginnings not endings and they are intended to open up issues not close them down.

Each chapter offers a modest case study of an aspect of young children's authorship. They are not designed to show examples of 'good' work, nor are they sets of practical hints for how to teach writing. Rather, they represent suggestions for ways of observing, and reflecting upon, how young children function as authors. The chapters follow a crudely chronological order, although this is not meant to imply any relationship between age and performance; indeed similar topics occur with several different age groups.

In **Chapter 1** Jeanne Price offers us a convincing demonstration that although nursery age children lack many conventional literacy skills, there is no excuse for restricting their opportunities to engage in the serious production of print. She tells us how a group of three- and four-year-old children entered into a written dialogue with a fantasy character (although it may not have been fantasy to them). In engaging in this dialogue, the children were able both to demonstrate what they knew about authorship and, at the same time, gain significant new experience of what participation in written dialogue actually involves.

In **Chapter 2** Mike Robinson offers us a very special perspective on young children's authorship; that of a parent. In one sense his is a naive contribution in that it comes, unlike all the others, from someone who has no professional concern with the education of young children. However, his perspective is, in reality, anything other than naive. In his examination of his son Joseph's play with language, he points out how the ability of $2\frac{1}{2}$-year-old Joseph to comment on his own and other objects' actions using specialised language forms, a variation on the 'fictionalisation of self', is an important part of emergent authorship. It also highlights the significance of book reading in providing experience upon which emergent writers can draw.

Vivienne Rowcroft, in **Chapter 3**, examines the extent to which children aged four and five are confident in their abilities as authors and are prepared to take risks with what they know. She examines the early letters of the children in a way which allows us to consider the willingness of young children to negotiate the selection, transmission, and presentation, of their information. In her examination of the special kinds of authorial moves being made by the children she demonstrates how children are able to orchestrate many decisions about the texts they are generating.

The dialogue journal between Rose Duffy and five-year-old Aileen in **Chapter 4** is a document recording the shifts in style as Aileen realises that her teacher really does want to write to her as a person rather than as a pupil. As the child becomes convinced of this so she changes from a pupil respondent to an initiator and equal participant in the dialogue. The dialogue journal allowed both her and her teacher to find new voices in the way in which they corresponded.

Jill Pauling in **Chapter 5** allows us to overhear a group of five- and six-year-old children in a Hong Kong classroom while they discuss and produce sets of rules. She reveals that what may be seen by some as an apparently minor authoring activity is actually an incredibly powerful meaning-making, intellectual experience for the children. Collaboration between the children allowed ideas to be generated, exchanged, negotiated, refined, and finally put onto paper. The extent of intellectual effort would never have been apparent simply from looking at the completed text.

Sue McCaldon and Linda Jones in **Chapter 6** investigate their four-, five- and six-year-old children's views about professional authors and authorship. They find that their children have many and varied views, but all of them are attempting to sort out in their minds the question of what counts as authorship.

A somewhat neglected aspect of authorship is the composition of items for notice-boards. Albeit often slight items, as a genre they have their own characteristics. In **Chapter 7** Janette Shearer traces the development of her five-year-old children's class notice-board, and documents the kind of usage made of it by the children.

In **Chapter 8** Anne Robinson investigates why the five- and six-year-old children in the class she taught for a year seemed reluctant to move beyond re-tellings of established tales. She suggests that the reluctance of her class sprang from a failure to realise that stories could be made up in the mind, and that once this realisation had been achieved there was a sudden flowering in the capacity of the children to write imaginative stories.

Georgina Herring persuaded a group of parents to collaborate with her class of six-year-olds in writing stories for younger children. In **Chapter 9** she focuses on the talk that accompanied the composition of the text and examines the role of the parents in helping the children get on the inside of an interesting and important authoring experience.

In **Chapter 10** Susan Williams recounts how she used book reviews as a way of helping her children focus on their own craft as writers. As the children developed book reviewing abilities, so they used them to reflect upon their own stories.

Nancy Pearson, our only American contributor, was possibly the first teacher in the United States to possess a copy of the Ahlbergs' *The Jolly Postman*. In **Chapter 11** she shows how she made this the base for offering the seven-year-old children in her second-grade class a whole variety of authoring experiences as they produced their own complete versions of *The Jolly Postman*.

Mary Greaves, in **Chapter 12**, takes us back to stories, talk and collaboration. The themes that run through so many of the chapters reappear here. The four six- and seven-year-old children whom she writes about found authorship an intensely interactive event. As they authored so they discussed, supported, criticised, encouraged, commented and analysed. They collaborated in highly effective and responsible ways when creating stories for younger children.

In all these chapters it is not the quality of the final text which is the important feature; in many cases the texts are nothing special or are even somewhat weak. The significant feature is the way the children reveal that they are reflective when generating their texts. They show a sensitivity to the constraints of written language which must dispel any notions that young children's writing is just 'talk written down' or that young children are incapable of making sensitive authorial decisions. These chapters reveal that practices which offer children the opportunity to take responsibility for their writing facilitate authorship and that authorship can only develop with experience of authorship. The children, whose work and thoughts we are privileged to observe in this book, offer us a most convincing demonstration that they are authors. They may be inexperienced authors but nevertheless just like more experienced professional authors when generating texts they think about what they are doing, why they are doing it, and what they are going to do with it.

Throughout this book we see children writing authentically, for real audiences and real purposes; we see children collaborating in very subtle ways to produce effective products; we see children using their space and time to experiment with, take risks with, and explore, meanings; we see children unafraid to take control of their own learning processes; we see children handling written language with sensitivity and care. We see authors at work.

Reference

Bennett, N., Desforges, C., Cockburn, A. and Wilkinson, B. (1984) *The quality of pupil learning experiences*: Lawrence Erlbaum Associates.

— I — The Ladybird letters
Jeanne Price

I was recently invited to a school to talk with the teachers about letter writing with young children. The teachers had been doing some letter writing with the children and I was there to discuss the results with the staff. The school had a nursery class and I suggested that we began our discussion with what had happened in this class. There was a long silence and then the nursery teacher said 'Oh but the children in the nursery can't write letters so we didn't include them'.

It is certainly the case that if we approach nursery or kindergarten children with the expectation that they can construct a conventional letter then we are going to be disappointed. But is this a sufficient reason for excluding letter writing from the nursery class? I do not think so. My own teaching with three- and four-year-olds had convinced me that children were, on the whole, intensely interested in print. I had also found that they were not inhibited in their interests by any failure to understand or use conventional ways of place holding meaning. I was also convinced that part of the learning process was facilitated by exposure to, interactions with, and demonstrations from, adults.

I believed very strongly that although I could not turn nursery children into conventional letter writers I could provide experiences which would illuminate for them some of the features involved in becoming the authors of letters. I felt it should be possible to provide young children with demonstrations of what it means to be a letter writer, to provide opportunities for children to show us what they do know about letter writing, and for me to respond to the marks they made as serious attempts to try to understand what is involved in being a letter writer.

The children in my nursery unit were aged three and four. The unit had been one of the nursery units involved with the Manchester section of the National Writing Project. As a consequence, the classroom was oriented to writing: there was a writing corner; there were many kinds of writing instruments and materials and the children's writing was displayed wherever possible (but nearly always in relation to some other work the children had been doing). Thus, the writing was contextualised by the activity to which it related. Most of the children in the class saw writing as just another interesting and fun option for them to carry out. They were interested to explore meanings in writing and all their work was valued and praised. The children had, for the most part, long gone past the stage where they said they couldn't write because they didn't know how.

Writing had been embedded into many activities within the classroom, in particular into structured play areas. Through these activities I had become aware that the children knew much more about writing than I had previously considered possible. I had not been prepared for the commitment and enthusiasm, nor had I expected the volume or quality of the responses they actually produced.

The dialogue

The children and I had been reading Eric Carle's *The Bad Tempered Ladybird* (in the United States, *The Grouchy Ladybug*). Following our readings the children had constructed a large model of a ladybird and set the model surrounded by trees and plants. They appeared to be prepared to collude in the idea that the ladybird was real and constantly talked about it as if it was real, made things for it and had conversations with it.

I decided that here was my opportunity to initiate some letter writing and see what the children's reaction would be.

A few days later when they came into the classroom a letter was waiting for them. It was not pointed out to them but one of the children soon found it and they all wanted to know what it said. I read it with a small group and between us we worked out the message of the letter. Within a few minutes it had been read by those children to every child (and every adult) in the classroom.

> The Magic Tree
> Beaver Road
> Nursery
>
> Dear Children
>
> Hello, I'm the ladybird who lives in the magic tree.
>
> Can you guess my name?
> Write with your ideas.
>
> Bye.

Example 1

There was a certain amount of intrigue. 'How could the ladybird write a letter?' One of the children speculated that it could write with its antennae and that seemed to be accepted. I told the children that if they wanted to reply they knew where all the materials were, and that if they did reply they could put their letter up on the board by the side of the ladybird. How would they respond?

The children responded with copious amounts of written material containing a range of suggestions:

Sarah suggested 'Philip', and quite reasonably used some of her limited knowledge of sound/symbol relationships to represent the name.

Example 2

One of the suggestions made (by Michael) was that the ladybird's name was Joe. After discussion it was agreed that this was a good name. It also had the advantage of being either a male or female name.

Example 3

It was very important to me that the notion of letter writing with which I was working was that of a letter exchange. Although people certainly do write a lot of letters which are 'one-offs' there is so much more to be experienced when a dialogue develops through a series of letters. I wanted to encourage this sense of there being a relationship between the letters. So, as the essence of a dialogue is that there is a sequence of exchanges, the ladybird, of course, wrote back.

The Magic Tree
Beaver Road
Nursery

Dear Children,
It was lovely to read all your letters and enjoy all of your drawings. One of you has very cleverly guessed my name — Joe. I hope you like it.

It is my birthday tomorrow and I am looking forward to opening my cards.

love,

Joe x x x

Example 4

In the ladybird's letter I tried to incorporate the features of a letter that related to maintaining a dialogue. The letter referred to the previous exchange and offered a subject for a future exchange. Thus, the cohesive and coherent nature of dialogue is represented within my teacher-written letter and, without instructing, I was trying to offer a demonstration about how a particular form of print works.

The responses were not simply written responses. Quite a few of the responses were cards or gifts for Joe.

Emma responded to the content of Joe's letter by making him/her a book, the front cover of which is reproduced opposite.

Example 5

The interest generated by the letter writing encouraged some children who had been more nervous about writing to commit themselves to print. Souren was inspired to write his first ever letter.

Souren's letter may be short but it nevertheless contains some significant features of a letter. It has the salutation, it has a content in the form of a drawing and it has both a closure and a signature.

Example 6

Jessica is another child drawn into the authoring of a letter by the excitement generated by the ladybird's letters.

Example 7

We do not know what Jessica's letter says but she has clearly understood that there has to be a content, that it has to have letters within it and she has set out to generate a message using those letters she knows. She also manages to include a new central concept – the name 'Joe'. Thus, she is able to generate messages but restrict herself to known forms, which is central to the use of an alphabetic system of writing (bearing in mind we only have twenty-six letters to generate everything we write).

The ladybird's next letter again looked both back and forward:

The Magic Tree
Beaver Road
Nursery

Dear Children,
            Thank you all
for my lovely party, cards and
presents. I really enjoyed the
Dolly Mixtures.
        Emily asked me how old I am.
Well I am 4 but I cannot work
out how old I will be next
year! Do you know?
        Thank you again,
        love
        Joe X X X

Example 8

Joel responds very simply but accurately telling him 'Joe you are going to be 5'. Joel gives evidence here of his interest in letters and sounds; his contribution is quite readable.

Joel

UJoeo 9Te5

Example 9

Matthew doesn't need words or letters for his message. His meanings can be placeheld quite succinctly using numbers. He can tell Joe that he is four but that he will be five. The message is incorporated within a drawing which in itself contains messages – all the kisses for Joe.

Example 10

The communication is simple but to the point. All the time, the children are being exposed to certain central features of written communication, in particular that it is about the exchanging of messages or information of some kind. I stress the importance of this because I am convinced that for many very young children a letter is no more than an envelope with a piece of paper in it – a kind of gift.

The ladybird's letters continued to arrive:

The Magic Tree
Beaver Road
Nursery

Dear Children,
                Did you have a good weekend? I did reading all your letters but I still do not know how old I will be next year. Simon said 4 and someone else said 7. Are these ages right? Please write and tell me.

love,
Joe

X X X

Example 11

The letters also provided an opportunity to hide some mathematical experiences. Emily responds with what must be seen as a perfect, simple piece of communication.

Emily's letter is short, sharp and absolutely to the point. The Plain English Campaign would approve of it.

Example 12

All this talk of birthdays leads to something new, not a simple response to a question previously asked but the generation of a new message, 'Joe you can come to my party'. Even casual inspection will demonstrate that not only does the child understand the function of writing a letter but has considerable control over the means by which one does it. There are clear sound symbol relationships being used, quite accurately, in this four-year-old's letter. Once one separates out the words, the effectiveness of the child's use of these relationships is clear. 'Party' is rendered 'PT', 'can' is 'KN', 'come' is 'CNM', and 'to' and 'my' are correct.

Example 13

Again Joe's letter seeks to maintain dialogue:

The Magic Tree
Beaver Road
Nursery

Dear Children,
        So I will be 5
next year. Does that mean I
can go into the Infant School
with you? Who will be my new
teacher? And who else will be
in my class?
                love
                Joe
                X X X

Example 14

It evokes a very complex response from Helen who is clearly one of the most experienced writers in the class. She is able to tell Joe that he will be going into the infant's school next year and that she will be going as well. She has responded to the question and generated a new element of text.

To Joe. you. Will. nxt. yeo
I can go IN the
Infants
Helen

Example 15

One morning there was no letter from Joe. Joel wanted to know why the ladybird hadn't written so I explained that Joe may get tired sometimes. Joel decided to help out and, in turn, other children decided to help him. Joel and friends decided what should be said and I wrote it down for them, after which they copied it. Joel did the copying while two friends helped him keep his place.

The magic Tree
Beaver Road
Nursery
Dear children
It was
lovely to read all your
letters. I liked my party
I enjoyed   the dominoes
best
love Joe
+ XTXXXXX+XX+XXXX

Example 16

It is a great pity that I do not have a recording of the conversation that took place while this was being carried out. The effort took about thirty minutes and I suggested half way through that they might like to take a rest and come back to it, but no, Joel was adamant that he wanted to complete it.

This raises the question of the extent to which the children actually believed in the ladybird as a writer. Occasionally a child would joke with us that one of the teachers was writing the letters, but at other times they seemed to have no doubt that it was possible. Perhaps they were hedging their bets. If they did not believe it then it couldn't write anymore.

Perhaps they believed in its reality rather in the way they talked and played with favourite dolls or teddy bears. I do not know the answer to this question but whatever the belief it did not interfere with the acceptance of writing to Joe as a legitimate activity.

The exchange continued for some time. Letters were exchanged about twice a week and the whole project went on for about six weeks.

Example 17

In the letter above the ladybird introduces the children to a new way of writing, one that some may have seen before in comics, but one which would probably be unfamiliar to most children of that age. Would the children take it up?

Joe received numerous
letters like this one.

Example 18

Joel, however, managed to
extend the form.

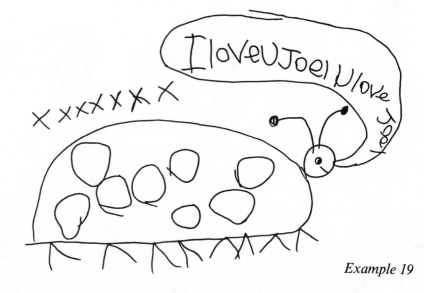

Example 19

The particular significance of this is not simply that it is a new way of handling text but that in its developed form, as in Joel's bubble talk, it introduces the children to the notion of another voice within writing.

In Joel's picture it is not really Joel talking but the ladybird talking to Joel. It is difficult for young children to understand that different voices can operate within text. By using bubble talk, one can introduce a fundamental aspect of speech punctuation, that of separating out the 'saying' from the reference to who is 'saying'. In other words the bubble is a form of speech mark. I am not in any way trying to claim that the children were ready for punctuation, but nevertheless a principle relating to the identification of voices within text was being introduced.

Conclusion

I have been able to show you only a minute selection of the responses made by the children. The letters and the responses were made into a huge book containing something like fifty A2 size pages. Quite clearly it had been a wonderful experience for the children. Not just because it was fun (and it certainly was that) but because through the work the children had gained significant insights into the nature, form and conventions of written dialogue.

The children were discovering what it meant to author a text that enabled messages to be passed between people, and they were being initiated into a form of dialogue that takes place in writing. They now knew so much more about the 'what', 'when' 'where', 'how' and 'why' of literacy and in particular letter writing.

This chapter originates from work carried out during the development phase of the SCDC National Writing Project 1986–88 © SCDC Publications 1988.

— 2 — Bookspeak

Mike Robinson

Introduction

Two things persuaded me to write this chapter. First, like most parents, I enjoy talking (and writing) about my own children, and the invitation to write about my $2\frac{1}{2}$ year-old son was irresistible. Second, because I write as a parent rather than any kind of educational specialist, I am able to indulge my own ideas without the responsibility that usually attaches to the professional. Both of these reasons are selfish, I know, but taken together they are singularly compelling. They even allow me to admit that my remarks stem from random observation and armchair reflection rather than from any systematic case study research. Like most parents I merely observe the progress of my children out of interest and concern. Insofar as I intervene in the process, my intervention is relatively unaffected by the trappings of educational theory, the identification of educational goals, or the informed application of educational methods. For the most part, I fly by the seat of my pants in dealings with my children, accepting that I will make mistakes but choosing to believe that I will more often be right than wrong. At the same time I must confess that I am fortunate that much of my social life is spent in the company of more expert educators. This means that in addition to reflecting on the development of my children, I have the opportunity to share these reflections with wiser heads.

My intention is to describe some of the features of language use which my son has developed. I will want to argue that they display a grasp of language functions which is more sophisticated than most adults, and many educators, are prepared to allow. I believe they signify a phase of development, which I shall call proto-literacy, in which the child has grasped some important ideas about literacy without being able, in any conventional sense, to read and write.

Proto-literacy

I believe that young children bring to all their learning processes an inherent capacity for creative experiment. It is only as they grow older that this capacity becomes dulled by repeated adult correction, or counter-demonstration: we teach our children to do things properly! For many behaviours, of course, this kind of homogenisation may be both necessary and useful. However, for other behaviours it is potentially destructive, and only a few individuals rediscover their creative capacities with a much later sharpening of critical faculties and a widening of experiential horizons. Young children display this creative predisposition particularly well in transactions with language. They are able to bring together a developing imagination and a growing base of experience in a way which permits adults to see the evidence of growth and change. As the command of language grows, the propensity to experiment in a variety of different ways grows with it. Long before they can read and write children develop the urge for exploration at the interface of imagination, experience, and language. Of course, the messages they produce lack the qualities which adults demand from 'conventional' communications: they are apparently unstructured, disjointed, inconsistent and, to an informed adult mind, perhaps literally inconceivable. Yet, to the child, it appears that they reflect something of a universe of possibilities which is not yet hampered by the need to take cognisance of adult rules of space and time, of physics, or of the full complexities of adult social relationships and networks. The problem for the educator is to preserve the child's creative intent in the face of a growing recognition of the orderliness of an 'objectified' reality.

This problem, I suspect, lies close to the core of the difficulties which adults face in introducing literacy to early learners. This is because text presents a threat as well as an opportunity. The threat stems from the possibility that the child will come to believe that only sense which is preserved in print can have any lasting value. By identifying an environment of 'real' authorship, from which the child is excluded, the urge to externalise his/her creative capacities in words may be seriously impeded. The motivation to explore and develop the literary skills of control, structure and refinement may be lost, and although the child may still emerge as a capable, and even sensitive, reader of text, as a writer he/she may have no more ambition than a scribe.

Just as the unimaginative handling of printed text and early writing can present a threat, I am sure that skilled handling opens up massive opportunities, some of which are specifically related to the notion of authorship. The most important of these, I think, is not related to the development of skills but rather to the abstract idea of intention. I would argue that it is in the matter of intention that the process of authorship is substantially defined. For the child, the existence of printed text can be used to confirm both the possibility and the value of preserving deliberately conjured utterances. Printed text, in other words, can convince the child of the possibilities of authorship. In the long term this can serve as a goal, or an aspiration for the fulfilment of creative ambitions, as well as encouraging the vital appreciation of print as a vehicle for the transmission, retention, and retrieval of ideas. In the shorter term, the sensitive introduction of text can offer access to demonstrations of language use which stimulate wider horizons and the extension of language skills, and which promotes the more effective correlation of words, experience, and imagination. In particular, by revealing the protocols and conventions of text, by showing them to be different from the reflexive and open-ended character of casual speech, the adult can help reveal to the child whole new areas of experiment and exploration. I would suggest that although the bulk of this task falls inevitably to professional teachers, some of the groundwork can be laid very early, before the child can read or write, during the phase that I am calling proto-literacy.

There are a number of qualities in both language and text which can be realised intuitively by young children. As these realisations develop, the child can display a grasp of 'literacy' that is only inhibited by the inability to read and write independently. Observation of my 2½ year-old son indicated at least a rudimentary grasp of the following characteristics of language and text:

- He knows the separate symbols which constitute our alphabet and is familiar with the sounds that are associated with them. Sometimes, like many children, he confuses 'b' and 'd' and 'p' and 'q' but, also like many children, he appreciates the potential for confusion and readily accepts sensitive correction.

- He knows that these individual symbols can be combined in various ways to form extended symbols called 'words'. He enjoys sounding out the letters in printed words but, although he can recognise, and even spell, a few simple words like 'Joe', 'cat', 'dog', 'it', 'at' and 'in', he cannot 'read' in a sustained sense.

- He appreciates that extended combinations of words create meanings and that the meanings published in his books have a quality of permanence: it is not possible to shorten the text of his favourite stories without being told, 'No Daddy, it doesn't say that, it says . . .'

- He can be observed searching for the most appropriate form of words to articulate his own spoken messages: frowns of concentration, pauses, and restarts often mark his grasp for precision within the limits of his vocabulary. He is aware, in other words, that for his audience the quality of a message varies with the selection and ordering of the words used to represent it.

- Like all young children he has been aware for a long time that the quality of messages can be altered or amplified by tone, volume, speed of articulation and so on, and he expects these qualities of spoken language to be employed when he listens to written language read aloud. 'No, Daddy,' he will say, 'the Fat Controller *shouts*'.

- He has begun to 'objectify' language, to see it as a vehicle for playful experiment and exploration. Sometimes he will speak in an exaggerated parody of 'standard English'; sometimes he will employ a 'thickened' version of the heavily accented speech of his home in Oldham. He pushes his 'pronunciation games' to the limits of comprehension, searching for the boundary between the still meaningful and meaningless. He plays, too, with construction and it is here that the influence of authored text becomes most apparent. He sometimes chooses to talk like a book!

Bookspeak

Thursday is my day with Joe. We visit places, do odd jobs, go swimming, or simply pass the time with play, TV, or books. On a cold and rainy January day we visited Manchester's Science Museum. The principal attraction was the collection of old steam locomotives which, we hoped, would be like Thomas The Tank Engine, or at least like one of his friends. Towards the end of our visit though, we moved to a section housing aeroplanes. The building had an upstairs gallery and protruding from the gallery at one point we could see the blue underside of a large aeroplane cockpit. I paid little attention to it, concentrating instead on the ancient flying machines in our immediate vicinity. Suddenly I felt Joe pulling my sleeve. I looked down to see him staring up at the cockpit and pointing. Then he said, quite distinctly, ' "What's that blue thing up there, Daddy?" said Joseph pointing.' I confess that I was a little taken aback, but I tried to enter into the spirit of things by saying, ' "It's the front of the aeroplane Joseph," Daddy replied.'

As our inspection continued I wondered about the unusual verbal construction that Joseph had used. I realised that it was another of his little games with words and, from time to time, I encouraged him to play it again. The exchanges went something like this:

Daddy: 'What's that thing up there Joe?' asked Daddy.
Joseph: 'Another aeroplane,' said Joseph.

and

Daddy: 'What colour is that one?' asked Daddy holding Joseph up.
Joseph: 'Its a red one,' replied Joseph.

The remainder of the afternoon passed pleasantly with occasional exchanges of the kind he had spontaneously started. They have continued since, not often and not intensively, but simply as an intermittent variation in the routine exchanges between parent and child.

The specific origins of this book-talk game, like the origins of other verbal games he plays, must remain a matter for speculation. To me, they seem to grow out of his early fascination with Thomas The Tank Engine and, particularly with the authority figure of the Fat Controller. This began when Joseph had his first Thomas book, at the age of about twenty months, and it was reinforced by the purchase and playing of *Thomas The Tank Engine* videos. Noisy episodes in the house, particularly involving his younger brother John Henry, were frequently interrupted by Joseph's cry of ' "Silence," said the Fat Controller'. On other occasions he would declare, ' "I cannot allow it" said the Fat Controller'. Mimicking the policeman in *Thomas In Trouble*, he told an aunt, 'You are a danger to the public'.

From here it is a relatively short step to the composition of the more elaborate compound sentences which are one of the distinguishing marks of written prose. The significant shift that Joseph had made by the age of two-and-a-half was in abandoning the phrases learned from books and substituting his own compound sentences in circumstances that were always wholly appropriate. For example, on one of the many occasions when his mother called him into the kitchen, he arrived with an exaggerated dash shouting, ' "I'm coming Mummy, I'm coming," exclaimed Joseph running as fast as he could'. Sometimes, of course, the sentence which results can be very confusing for an adult who is not expecting it. After a bout of 'flu' involving a visit from our GP, Joseph decided to play 'doctors'. He drew his small reclining chair to the foot of my armchair and began to 'examine' me: feet, hands, face, and finally, head. Then solemnly came: ' "What's the matter with your head Daddy?" the doctor wondered, said Joseph'.

The examples, not all as bizarre as this one, could go on and on, but reflecting on this book-talk game it appears that his contributions fall into two distinct categories. When the initiative comes from his mother, or from me, our comment usually takes the form of a question: 'Putting down the paper, Daddy asked, "What are you doing Joseph?" ' In these circumstances where he has little time for reflection or composition, his sentences rarely extend beyond a brief reply and an attribution: ' "I'm playing," said Joe.' Even so he has mastered a wide number of appropriate verbs: ' "Yes," Joseph declared', or 'insisted', or 'remarked', or 'replied', or 'shouted', or 'wondered', and so on. But, when he initiates the game his efforts are invariably longer, more complex, and more studied. They take on a very particular pattern which mirrors more vividly the language of books. The first element is usually the conversational content. The second element attributes the words, usually to himself, and the third element comments on the manner in which the words were spoken, or the actions and gestures that accompanied them. Moreover, it is quite clear that he is creating these complex sentences with a firm understanding of this function, and out of a clear appreciation of their origins in authored tales. Momentarily he becomes, as it were, both the author and a character in an episode of his own invention, something which many authors of fiction would understand perfectly.

This dual role was even more apparent as he sat eating breakfast one morning. In the kitchen next door his mother had switched on the washing machine and its dull, persistent whine, usually easily ignored, had obviously attracted his attention. Pausing between mouthfuls he tilted his head and said, ' "Is that an aeroplane I can hear?" he thought. "No I must be mistaken. It's just the washing machine".' In this case by abandoning the use of his own name and substituting a pronoun, he seemed to be distancing his roles as 'author' and 'character' still further. This was shown again as we sat around his play mat playing with toy cars and the like. The mat is inscribed with the plan of the village: it has roads, a school, a garage, a bank and so on. Running through the middle of the village is a river and it was into the river that Joseph chose to crash his Dinky aeroplane. 'Crash,' he said, and then: ' "I shall have to get the breakdown truck, I think," he said to himself.' Then a moment or two later: ' "Where can I hook it on to the plane?" he wondered.'

His delight when constructions like this evoke a positive response of amusement, pleasure or surprise, is very real and very strong. In effect he has conducted an experiment, in an atmosphere of playfulness, and its outcome has affirmed his initial hypothesis; that is, by employing a particular form of words he has successfully heightened responses to his message. He does the same thing with words themselves, sometimes trying out wholly new ones inspired by the irresistible logic of childhood. Travelling to the supermarket on a rainy day, for example, he looked down at his wellingtons and said, ' "It's a puddling day. I'll just have to splash in the puddles I suppose," said Joe.' It is surely no accident that he was then enjoying the story of *Alfie's Feet*.

The fact that Joseph has mastered these compound sentences is not, I believe, unusual. My guess would be that when most children relive tales in their imagination they internalise language constructions of a similar kind. The unusual feature is that Joseph articulates them and adapts the context of the sentence to the everyday circumstances in which he finds himself, making a game of the constructions he devises. Even the emergence of the game, though, was a fortuitous matter: I simply happened to be there when he tried it out, and on that particular day I had the time and the patience to respond positively. On other days, and in the routine chaos of a busy household, I might never have noticed. By encouraging in him a sense of achievement, however, and by a little gentle reinforcement he was persuaded to pursue his game, in public, and with the willing vigour which the young sometimes display when finding the approbation of the old.

I believe that his willingness to contribute to this exploration of book language is related to his general understanding of story as a whole. Here, though, there is an important inconsistency. On the one hand he appears to believe that characters in stories are 'real' characters and he is disappointed when 'real' locomotives fail to display the face of Thomas, or a Gordon, or a Daisy but, on the other hand, he will sometimes laugh at the suggestion that a storybook animal might talk. Moreover, although he insists that the language of some stories should never change, he is quite willing for others to be altered. His rules appear to be simple: favoured stories which are consistently pleasing are sacrosanct; stories which are not pleasing must never be repeated and must even be removed from his bedroom. Stories which are pleasing in some points but unpleasing in others may, however, be radically recast. Taken together these responses suggest that his understanding of story, though not fully developed, involves the beginning of an appreciation of the control that the storyteller can exercise over the events in their tales.

A good example of this came when I feigned ignorance and asked him to recount *The Tale Of Peter Rabbit*. It is, I should say, a tale with which he is very familiar. I recorded the version which Joseph told to me and so it is quite easy to locate the changes which he brought to Beatrix Potter's original text. For example, Peter ate only cucumbers (Joseph's favourite vegetable) and 'chips and carrots'. Mr McGregor doesn't mind in the slightest when Peter eats his cucumbers; 'it's a yes' as Joseph puts it. Peter's father is not shot by Mr McGregor but actually goes to visit him for a talk. Despite the apparent friendliness of the McGregors and the rabbits, however, neither Peter Rabbit nor his father returns to the garden but in future buy their cucumbers at ASDA! By contrast, Joseph's version of *Toby And The Stout Gentleman*, adheres scrupulously to the Rev. Audrey's text.

This willingness to alter stories which contain threatening or unpleasant episodes, like the death of Peter Rabbit's father or James the Red Engine's crash with the tar waggons, helps to confirm the views that he has some real, if unconscious, grasp of the storyteller's role. This grasp is reinforced, perhaps, by another verbal game which we play. This game involves the invention of a story with the sequential addition of a sentence by each participant. Thus:

Daddy: Once upon a time there was an elephant . . .
Mummy: The elephant went for a long walk . . .
Joseph: He went to the seaside . . .

and so on. As these stories develop it is clear that Joseph cannot yet sustain images of an extended sequence of related events and, in adult terms, his contributions rapidly become disjointed and shapeless. Yet he perseveres, seeing the world in his own terms and holding interest in the game for several minutes. This suggests that in addition to having grasped some of the style of book language, there are the beginnings of an appreciation of an authored tale in his mind. The task for the future is to encourage the flowering of this appreciation and to help him develop the abilities needed to control, exploit and manifest it.

Epilogue

We were driving in the car to collect Joseph's younger brother, John Henry, who had spent the day with his grandmother. An exchange occurred which went like this:

Daddy: Let's collect the Slug from Grandma's ('Slug' is a nickname given to John Henry because of his tendency to salivate copiously as he crawls, leaving a distinctive trail on the carpet).
Joseph: No let's collect the Biter (The 'Biter' is another nickname given to John Henry for very obvious reasons).
                   (*Pause*)
Joseph: 'Let's collect the Biter of the victim' said Joseph, smiling.

— 3 — Young letter writers as authors
Vivienne Rowcroft

Introduction

At the beginning of the school year I had taken a temporary post as coordinator for the Rochdale section of the National Writing Project. For the first time I found myself not a class teacher. Although the role of coordinator offered opportunities for examining children's development as writers, as well as deepening my own understanding of writing development, it also took me away from permanent contact with my primary source of data, the children. I wanted very much to maintain regular contact with children but the demands of my new post were going to make this very difficult. The solution seemed to be to engage in an aspect of written communication which allowed for some distancing between the participants. I decided, therefore, to maintain contact with a group of new reception children by becoming a correspondent with them through letter writing.

I began my association recognising that I needed to do four things:

- Discuss my hopes and aims with the children and class teacher.
- Explain the project to the children's parents.
- Introduce the children to the activity of writing letters.
- Identify a way of analysing the moves the children made as authors of letters.

The class teacher was highly supportive of the project – indeed it would have been impossible without her full involvement. As a result of discussions about the children's authorship we decided that it could only happen fully if we created an environment which supported, in many ways, the children's literate development. This involved setting up a writing corner with free access to a variety of materials and implements to allow for experimentation; the introduction of 'open entry' activities which provided children with the space to show us what they knew about writing; the provision of literacy-related materials into structured play areas; the creation of print-rich displays around the classroom; the adding, to the book corner, of newspapers, magazines and comics; and valuing children's work by displaying it as frequently as possible and in as many different ways as possible.

We discussed the teacher's role as a 'facilitator'; involving the use of discussion, helping the children plan and think about what they were going to write, encouraging the children to have a go at spelling, encouraging them to find their own solutions, and responding as a genuine audience for the children's work rather than just as a teacher assessor.

I had a meeting with the parents of the children with whom I was going to work. We talked about the kind of writing that the children had already done at home. They all agreed that the children had 'copied', pretended to fill in 'forms', pretended to write 'notes' etc. It was clear, however, from the parents' comments that they viewed these activities as separate from the teaching of writing. One mother captured the spirit of the rest when she said, 'I never tried to teach her to write, only her name, because I was frightened I'd do it wrong and confuse her for when she came to school.' I requested their help directly in the letter writing, asking them to find time to share the letters with the children if they were brought home and, if the children felt that they wished to write letters, perhaps the parents would make it possible by providing materials and help if the children needed it.

The letter exchange

I discussed letter writing with the children, introducing it by reading the Ahlbergs' *The Jolly Postman*. The children certainly had some notions about the nature of letters:

> 'It's a postcard'
> 'An invitation'
> 'An envelope'
> 'A card'
> 'The postman brings it'.

These answers were, however, all concerned with the physical nature of the letter as an object. I presented the class with a giant postcard:

> Dear children
> I really miss seeing you every day. Perhaps you will
> write and tell me what you have been doing.
> Love from
> Miss Rowcroft

We read the postcard and there was immediate agreement to my request that they write to me. I explained that I was not going to write it for them and that I wanted it to be their own writing. I told them it did not matter to me if it was not like 'grown ups' writing as I would, nevertheless, be able to understand it.

Unlike other classes with which I had worked, there was no panic or worry about starting to write. Perhaps this was because these children were, through the kind of support and provision discussed above, able to view themselves as successful writers rather than failures. The questions I received were about the form of the letter:

'Where does 'Dear' go?'
'What do I write at the top?'
'Where does 'love' go?'
'Where do I put my name?'

The questions this time related to the form and it was noticeable that none of the children asked questions which suggested that they did not know how to say something or know what to say.

After settling the initial questions the children wrote their letters using a variety of different strategies. I was not anticipating that the children would respond by offering me a formally laid out letter. I was content to accept as a letter any attempt at explicit written communication from the writer to the reader.

Victoria copied my letter but understood the exercise well enough to alter the names.

> Dear miss Rowcroft
> I really miss seeing yuo every day
> Perhaps you win write to me and
> tell me whate you have been doing
> Love from
> Victoria Cowrad

Example 1

Scott knew exactly what he was going to say: 'My mummy is poorly in bed'. He used the letters he knew well, those in his own name, to produce his message.

> Sco C () ntts roctsi
> S c ott StOlotOttsi
> S C Ott

Example 2

Some used their knowledge of letter/sound relationships to produce words: 'I like my bike'.

> Deqr miss Rowcroft
> ILqc Mq bk
> Leve carrie-Ann

Example 3

Some used random letters:
'I do a lot of painting'.

Dear mISS Rowjroft
pioslopA
Lovefrom   .
Rhiannon

Example 4

Only two would make no attempt and I wrote for them. I did not ask
them to copy as this was superfluous to the exercise.

What did these first letters tell me about these children as authors of a
particular kind of text? The majority were confident in their ability as
authors and were willing to take risks with what they knew. They
understood that writing is about forming symbols on paper to capture a
message. They used signs recognisable as letters rather than scribbles.
Some were able to show and use their knowledge of letter/sound
relationships; they could be heard attempting to spell out words using the
alphabet frieze for cues. Some had the concept of words being separate
units. They fulfilled the function of a friendly letter writer. They told me
something about themselves. I think their voices are there; it is them
speaking on the paper. By reading their unaided authored text I can see
something of what it is that they can do.

The importance of my last sentence is that too often what is on the
paper fails to inform the reader about anything other than minute bits of
information concerning the children's ability as authors. This point was
made clear when I compared the letters with some aided writing the
children had done just before the letter writing association.

Danielle's copy writing

I stayed in my
I. Stayed in my

house with Uncle
house with Uncle

Don and Nanna. At
Don and Nanna. At

night-time they
night-time they

went home.
went home.

Example 5

Danielle's copy writing reveals that she has good pencil control but tells me little else. I can only assume that the sentence is actually the one she said and has not been subtly modified by the teacher. I can only assume that she wrote from left to right. I can make no assumptions at all that she knows words are separate units and are separated by spaces. However this inability to judge this type of writing does not stop most parents and teachers being very satisfied with it simply because it looks neat.

I do a lot of drawing

Dear MiSS RoWCroft
I Da qlo fo Dong
Love from
.from x x x
Danelle Parkinson

Example 6

What the copy writing did not show is evident from the unaided writing. She clearly does separate words with spaces and she has an understanding that the sounds have a relationship to the letters. She can compose a perfectly acceptable message. The unaided text gives a good account of Danielle's knowledge about authoring text.

Jonathon's copy writing

This is my
rCm
chocolate machine. I
CD
put in Ip and the
chocolate zig-zags
down.

Example 7

Jonathon's copy writing seems to suggest he has no pencil control. In fact there appears to be no effort to actually copy the words. From this evidence it would be easy to dismiss him as a non-starter; not yet ready to write.

I like playing

Example 8

However, when responding to the genuine communicative situation he produces a text which forces a considerable revaluation of his competence (see Example 8). He still has problems with pencil control but compared with the first example there is a massive improvement, a difference that was even greater when he was later offered larger pieces of paper on which to write. His message shows he understands there has to be a relationship between sounds and symbols. Later, on a larger sheet of paper, he wrote:

I like reading books too

Example 9

He began to show me that he was possibly as far along the author's road as Danielle, although lacking her fine motor control. Some words he took from my letter and some were already within his spelling competence. The use of the word 'too' is perhaps the most significant aspect of this letter. With that single word he has turned a statement into a response. He demonstrates an awareness of an important aspect of maintaining dialogue; the picking up of previously written material.

The consequence of receiving the first letters was that I was inspired, delighted, and totally enthusiastic. I continued to exchange letters with the children on a weekly or twice weekly basis for the rest of the term.

The main difficulty for anyone looking at the efforts of people who have limited experience of writing is to be able to look at those efforts in such a way so as to fully understand the complexity of the authoring moves that are being made. There is too much of a temptation to treat them as simple pieces of work because, by conventional standards, they appear simple and are short.

I was fortunate in having available to me some ideas from the work of Jerry Harste (principally through Vargus 1983*). I cannot pretend to fully understand all of his work but it did give me an opportunity of exploring the children's writing in ways that recognised the children's responses as potentially complex and orchestrated authorial moves.

In essence, Harste offers a grid down one side of which are a number of psycho-social factors, and across which are a number of linguistic factors. Any one of the psycho-social factors can be examined in relation to any one of the linguistic factors.

	Pragmatics	*Semantics*	*Syntax*	*Grapho-phonemic*
Negotiability				
Textual intent				
Risk taking				
Fine tuning				

There is not space in this article to explore the use of the complete grid to analyse the response of the children in their letters. I am going to concentrate on the first psycho-social factor 'negotiability' and explore its association with the linguistic factors.

Negotiability

The selection of 'negotiability' is important, as through examining negotiability we have the opportunity to see whether children's responses are unreflective (and thereby indicating authorship in only the most cursory sense, if at all) or reflective (indicating care, selection and consideration in the choice of responses in relation to the nature of the activity; thus authorship in a most exact and demanding sense).

*Vargus, N.R. (1983) Socio-cognitive constraints in transaction: letter writing over time. Unpublished PhD thesis: Indiana University.

Negotiability can be defined as: 'The moves and shifts language users make in order to strike a contract, and the subsequent moves made in the selection, transmission and presentation of information across communication systems' (Vargus, 1983).

Negotiability and pragmatics

Before beginning letter writing the children have certain pragmatic choices to make. They could decide:

■   Whether to accept the social contract and write a letter.

■   Whether to modify or renegotiate the social contract and communicate in ways that seemed less letter-like.

■   Whether to reject the social contract and refuse to communicate.

■   What kind of social relationship should be established through the letter writing activity.

All the children were prepared to accept, at some level, the social contract and take part in the letter writing, although clearly the ways in which they decided to participate were different from each other; there was certainly some negotiation going on. Accepting the social contract at a basic level meant that they were prepared to continue as partners in letter writing, maintain the communication and follow, in general terms, the notion of letter writing.

The question needs to be asked, Why did they accept the social contract? The simple answer might be that it would have been difficult for them not to, even though my initial letter had stressed 'perhaps you will write and tell me what you have been doing'. Although it would have been quite acceptable to me to have children who did not wish to participate, it is very difficult to persuade children that, as a teacher-like figure, you really do not mind if they choose not to do something. Such real freedom of choice is rare in most classrooms. Children know that being at school is not an elective activity, and that much of the content of schooling is imposed upon children rather than negotiated. However, it is also clear that children 'play the game' and are often incredibly willing to go along with teacher-initiated suggestions, especially when there is a possible 'fun' tag associated with the activity.

It must also be remembered that these children were writers and not afraid of writing. Therefore, for most of them it was not an outrageous or uninteresting contract which they were being invited to accept.

Dear children

I reall

miss not seeing you

Carrie - Ann

Example 10

Although they all chose to accept the social contract the degree of acceptance differed. In the first exchange two of the children chose simply to copy the basic text of my letter. One of these was Victoria (see the first example in this article); another was Carrie-Anne (Example 10). Copying presented them with a predictable way of making sense in an unpredictable situation. When faced with adult script in school, children are used to copying it rather than generating a novel response to it. In other situations I have seen children cry and say 'I can't' because they have been invited to write something on their own. Victoria and Carrie-Anne negotiated the contract so that they could continue to participate in it. It would have been open to those children to have refused on the grounds that they did not know, or were not sure, what to do. Both exhibited a certain degree of risk taking in modifying the contract. Was it what I would accept? Both children later became generators of new content:

I like drawing

Example 11

Thank you for your letter I like my bike it is red

Example 12

Other children, as can be seen in the earlier examples, had no hesitation in accepting the invitation of my postcard and responded by telling me about themselves, although they used a variety of forms to do so.

For the second letter many of the children chose to modify the content by introducing an additional means of place-holding meaning, namely pictures. As adults, we do not normally associate drawing as being typical of the letter writing genre; however, for children it may reflect a best way to author a meaning.

Example 13

Writing to someone demands decisions regarding the degree of formality or distance or, conversely, the friendliness or hostility of the exchange. In this case a relationship already existed. The children seemed to regard me as a trusted adult, although almost certainly a teacher-type adult. Young children often find it easy to have a warm friendly relationship with their teacher and are used to sharing confidences and experiences, although this may reflect lack of experience in discrimination rather than a deliberate choice on their part. All the children used their first names to sign the letters but some used their surnames as well.

I do a lot of drawing

Example 14

By the second letter and for all following letters all the children used only their first names.

My nan was in hospital but she has come back

Example 15

I signed my letter to them 'Love Miss Rowcroft'. This seems rather formal but I believe that to the children this was my name rather than a formal title. Most of the children generally used kisses in the letters. When asked why they used kisses the children offered:

'because you love someone'
'to give something to someone'

or, less reflectively,

'because you put them'.

The letters throughout the exchange seemed to be between people who are real to each other and share a mutual trust.

Negotiability and semantics

When letter writing, certain semantic decisions need to be made. What meanings will I use and what communication system is the best method of capturing my meanings? In selecting meanings, letter writers have a number of choices to make:

■ To maintain – to stay with the correspondent's, or their own, topics and add minimally (if at all) to them (as in Example 1).

■ To expand – to use the correspondent's, or their own, topics and build on them but staying within the overall topic (for instance Example 9).

■ To generate – to introduce a completely new topic into the correspondence (as in Example 13).

Clearly the above categories, while involving semantic decisions, also imply different degrees of risk taking. The different categories of the system outlined above are not mutually exclusive; they interact in a coherent and holistic set of behaviours on the part of a child or, indeed, any author.

Some children used their drawings to maintain meanings, drawing them after they had written the text.

Thank you for your letters.
I'm going to play games

Dear Miss Rowcroft

Thank you for your letters. I'm going to ple goe

Lov from Danielle
x x

Example 16

Other children used their drawings to expand on their message. Mark wrote 'Mrs Sutton is my friend' and then drew a picture of her and her bed because she had recently been away ill.

Mrs Sutton is my friend

mrs sutton is my friend.

Love from mark x x
x

Example 17

Michael wrote, 'I like snow' and then offered, through his drawing, the reason why he liked snow.

I like snow

Example 18

For some children drawing opened the way for meaning making in ways that might have been inhibited if they had been restricted to using words. Some children drew first to place-hold their meanings. Their conversation reveals something of this process:

'Have you done the sun?'
'I've done it with spikes coming out.'
'I've nearly finished my drawing.'
'This is a football pitch. That's me playing football.'
'Now I'm going to write, 'Dear Miss Rowcroft'.'

Me playing football

Example 19

Similarly Jamie very carefully drew the picture of himself and his mother before producing the message, 'Mum and me in town'.

Mum and me in town

Example 20

It is clear that drawing is being used in quite different ways by these children. These particular children also moved around between those ways of using drawings. They chose whatever strategy seemed to be the most appropriate one for the occasion. As a way of generating meaning, holding on to meaning, and expanding meaning, the use of drawing was an integral part of the authorship of these children.

There will be people, including many teachers, who see this as something separate from being an author. They may like to reflect on what they read themselves, including this book and, in particular, this chapter. How would they get on with this chapter without the illustrations, which I am, by proxy, using to place-hold certain of my meanings? In some cases I have been given direction by the children's work; in others I have had ideas which have led me to search the children's work for examples. I seem to be working in exactly the same way as the children did when authoring their texts. The only difference is that I am using someone else's 'drawings'.

I think that the children are asking us to accept their drawing and writing as a whole. It is not that they fail to understand the distinction between drawing and writing; they do. It is that one complements the other. For children, their drawing is a vehicle for meaning in a text, just as drawing and illustration (including photography) are vehicles for meaning in adult texts. Michael might, or might not, have been able to write about his sledge (Example 18) but he chose to use drawing in a way that makes a special contribution to the reader's understanding of his text.

Negotiability and syntax

By the term syntax we mean not only grammar, but the rules by which print functions in particular contexts. Thus the form of a letter constitutes a type of syntax. An initial syntactical question is whether the children's writing is like written language; do they have a register for writing? Evidence for this can be gathered by observing what they write and also by what they do not put in their writing. Clearly the children did not normally go around saying 'Dear Miss Rowcroft'. Nor did they finish their conversations by signing off with 'love from . . .'. The children's questions noted earlier, 'Where does Dear go?', and 'Where does Love go?' are not the questions of ordinary conversation. Much of the initial content of the letters was in the form of simple statements: 'Mummy is poorly'; 'I like my bike'; or 'I like playing'. The fact that these may be said in speech does not necessarily mean that in the letters they are simply speech written down (although what is wrong with that–is not speech reflective?). One has to ask where do children learn that such a statement will do. Children seldom go up to anyone and say 'I like playing'. Children seldom talk in simple sentences; they tell you all about a subject but, when it comes to writing something down they demonstrate that they know that what is to be written has to be different from what is usually said. Experience with teachers who take what children say about a picture and generate a lifeless, truncated sentence such as 'Mummy is shopping' soon teaches children something about the characteristics of school writing. Similarly, experience of reading material which is restricted to 'reading scheme' books may also provide a certain restricted register for writing.

A consequence of the letter exchange was the freeing of some children from the chains of such restricted productions (for another very powerful example of this see the following chapter by Rose Duffy). Children who, at the start, were writing 'I like playing' were later generating their own topics:

My nana is coming Saturday. Daddy is meeting her

Dear MISS ROWCIft
INand is c lm sar
DaDDy meet she
Love from
car rie - Ah n
X Y

Example 21

Children who were, at the start, doing little more than copying my letter (see Example 1) were later writing:

My nana and grandad came
My nana washed up
Grandad watched television
Me and Andrew were in bed
I have been out

Dear. MissRowc.roft.
IM nanna and Grandad Came.
IM nanna Washd up
Grandad Wachd telvign
Me and Andrew in bed
I have been ont
Love from XX
Victoria.

Example 22

Paradoxically as the letters lengthened so, in some respects, they became a little more like speech. But how are the children to learn the subtle ways in which writers link topics and maintain topics unless they feel free to write more than one simple statement? Although the similarity to speech increased, not one of the children ever used some of the typical phenomena of speech; there are no 'ums' and 'ers' in their writing, yet I doubt whether anyone taught them that those bits belong only to speech.

Negotiability and the grapho-phonemic system

Writing conventionally places considerable constraints upon children. The child is, essentially, faced with two positions. The first is to limit what one wants to mean by only authoring that which one can represent in approved script. The second is to author what one wants to mean and disregard whether one knows how to script it conventionally. Of course, in practice, the child's response lies somewhere between the two, depending on how much experience the child has, whether the child is prepared to negotiate his/her desires with the demands of the system, and to what extent the child is prepared to be a risk taker. In other words, does one go towards the semantic demands or the orthographic demands?

The conventional response of the non-risk taking young child who places orthographic demands above semantic demands is, when faced with a request to author a text, either 'I can't', or a demand for something to copy. In the early stages of the exchange two children would not write on their own. Some, like Victoria, (Example 1) resolved the problem by borrowing an already approved set of representations but making minor changes. Some, like Scott, (Example 2) put semantic considerations above orthographic ones and lived happily with their own representations of messages.

As the sequence of exchanges progressed, so children like Victoria became less frightened of the activity and were more prepared to negotiate room to represent their meanings. Jamie is a good example of this. His work progressed from Example 3 to Example 23.

I hurt my nose
I fell off a massive stone

Example 23

He has moved from the representation of a very scheme-like sentence to something which, in its use of the word 'massive', demonstrates a certain amount of exploration. The fact that he cannot placehold the meaning in a conventional way has not inhibited him as a writer. He is prepared to author what he wants to mean rather than withdraw from authoring because he does not know how to write something.

Conclusion

This involvement in a letter writing exchange has convinced me that young children are authors and will continue to develop as authors if we give them the space, the time, a supportive environment, and genuine reasons for writing. It is clear to me that children are not unreflective in the ways they approach the crafting of a text. They all are capable of operating on many different levels and operating on several of those levels at any one time; in other words they orchestrate a response to the demands of authorship.

What they write may not always be recognisable in conventional terms but to dismiss those efforts as lacking in authorship is to diminish the powerful thought that has gone into the generation of a text. Of course, children will still need considerable experience of generating texts and of interacting with the texts of others, but high level skills are not acquired quickly; they need time to develop. To interfere and say that because children's work does not appear to be conventional means that authorship is too difficult for them is to miss the essential qualities of the things that children actually do. To replace those qualities by teacher-scripted exercises which take away from children the power to negotiate, risk take, fine tune and explore textual intent, and leave them as little more than copiers, is to demean children's intellectual performance as authors.

—4— Dear Mrs Duffy
Rose Duffy

Introduction

After two terms of schooling, the children in my class were authors of a kind. They seemed to have no problem in producing sentences like:

Anne (5yrs 3mths)

'Me and my mummy and my daddy and my baby are gong to my garns and garndad's and we are gong to have tea and then we will go hom to bed.'

Clare (5yrs 6mths)

'This is me and Lucy playing ball in me garden we whent in tehn we had tea then we whent home.'

Mark (5yrs 3mths)

'here ius me and Richard playing fut ball in my graden and my dad came home and we went to the park.'

Comments had often been made by parents and others that the children in this reception class wrote 'surprisingly well' and, indeed, displays of the children's stories were often highly commended by visitors to the classroom. Why then did I feel so dissatisfied? Was I expecting too much from these barely five-year-olds?

The reason for my frustration was the 'sameness' in the children's writing; they all tended to write in the same way. What was missing from the children's writing was the children themselves. The boring sentences sounded as if they had been borrowed from basal readers and did not seem to belong to the children. There was no hint, indeed no sign, in the writing of the individuality of the children; yet one only had to listen to them talking among themselves to be struck by their unique personalities. Why then did they all write in this 'cloned' fashion? Was it perhaps myself who was, unwittingly, the problem? Perhaps the children wrote as they did because I expected no different from them, or because the models of writing in their reading books were of this nature or because children who are learning to write simply do write like this?

Almost all of the children in the class were able to write comfortably in the 'cloned' fashion described earlier. Writing had been an important part of the day from the time the children started school, and all the children were used to writing daily. So much so, that writing had become an almost non-event causing neither distress nor excitement.

When I began to think back to those times when the children had become very involved and excited I remembered how at Christmas the children had brought cards which they had written out at home and how they had been enthusiastically posted in the school post box. They had obviously enjoyed this activity and I decided to resurrect the post box. Encouraged by their response I decided to make a more formal attempt to help the children to develop the personal quality in their writing by, hopefully, giving them a better audience with whom they could communicate.

Introducing dialogue journals

A few days later I invited the children to write to me. Each child was given a small book into which he/she could write, and into which I would reply. I decided to use a journal form of letter writing so that the results could be easily monitored. I felt that if actual letters were written, I might end up swamped by so many bits of paper that I would lose any sense of coherence and be unable to control what was going on.

There are some advantages in using dialogue journals with young children. The principal one is that all the exchanges exist in a permanent record which is always available to the children. There is a tendency, when exchanging letters with children, for them to mislay, lose, or throw away the letters, which can present difficulties when a child needs to respond to a particular letter, but does not have it to hand. Also, in a conventional letter writing exchange, the children would not have access to letters they had already written. Dialogue journals certainly make this aspect easier and the letters featured in this chapter contain evidence of a girl utilising the previous letters for spellings and ideas.

One major advantage of dialogue journals for young children is that it allows them to use the language of their speech. There is enormous pressure upon children to learn to write stories and, while the writing of stories may be beneficial for young children, it does pose some problems. They have to take their authorship into genres with which they may be only partially familiar. In dialogue journals children can write in a genre they know because they can use speech.

The dialogue journals

The rest of this chapter explores the effect this had on one child, and the effect it had on my understanding of what I was doing when I tried to help children develop distinctive styles as authors. The series of exchanges took place between myself and Aileen, a child aged five years and six months.

There were some rules involved. The children were not allowed to have any help and when they had finished writing, the books were to be left on the teacher's table, not shown to me. I would then take them home to respond to. So, although the dialogue was between two people who saw each other constantly, the actual messages were written and read apart. It may seem somewhat false for a child to be exchanging letters with a teacher who is in the same classroom, but the children, I believe, saw it rather differently. For them it was a chance to have a special dialogue with someone who was often occupied with other people. It was, in effect, a way of securing the attention of the teacher.

I would like to deal with the complete dialogue journal for a three week period. I started the exchange by putting a letter to the children on the blackboard and the children were given books in which to reply. From then on the exchanges were all in the books.

Dear mrs Duffy
I hop you had a
very nisc time af
the uter school
Love
From
Aileen

Example 1a

Dear Aileen,
I had a very nice time
at the other school
thank you. Did you have
a nice time with
Mrs Taylor ?
love from
Mrs Duffy

Example 1b

Dear mrs Duffy
I did have a
lovley time with
mrs talor Lots of
Love from Aileen

Example 1c

Dear Aileen

Thank you for your
letter. How is your
new baby? Does she
have any teeth yet?
Does she cry a lot?

love from
Mrs Duffy

Example 1d

Dear mrs Duffy
I am very happy
my baby dose not
have teeth yet She
dose cry a lot

Love from Aileen

Example 1e

Dear   Aileen

I   have   forgotten   her

name.   How   old   is   she

now   ?

love   from

Mrs   Duffy

Example 1f

Dear   mrs   Duffy
her   name   is

thres a   she   is   5   muneas
Lots   of   nice Lovefrom

Aileen

♡ ♡ ♡   ♡   ♡   ♡ ♡   ♡ ♡   ♡   ♡
x x x x x   x   x x   x x x x x x x

Example 1g

So far the exchanges are fairly conventional. They are better than the 'cloned' writing but, nevertheless, are very simple exchanges which do not reflect a distinct child's voice. Aileen seemed to have sorted out a register and was going to stick to it. My part of the dialogue was that of a typical teacher; I was asking all the questions. Aileen was behaving like a typical pupil; she answered all the questions but did not enter the dialogue with a novel contribution. One possible strategy to wean her away from this limited register would be to involve her with topics that were of more interest to her.

Dear   Aileen
            Who   does   Theresa
look   like ?   Do   you   hold
her   on   your   knee
sometimes ?
                  love   from
                  Mrs   Duffy
                        x x x

Example 2a

Dear   mrs   Duffy
threasy Looks   like
my   anute Angela

and   me   wenl
wos   a   baby
   and l do   on
   hold   her
my   knee
   love   from
      Ai leen
   ♡ ♡ ♡ ♡
   xx x xx

Example 2b

Dear   Aileen

Which   poems   do   you   like

best   in   your   new

poetry   book ?

love   from

Mrs Duffy

Example 2c

Dear   mrs   Duffy
I   like   piggy   on   the
Railway   it   is   a
nice   poem   i   like
the   poem   it   is   nice
It   makes   me happy
I   wont   to   yo to bed
I   like   my   Book
Very   mouts   my   hart
Strates   beting
I   like   it   very
Very   mouts   Lots
of   love   from
Aileen

Example 2d

Dear   Aileen

Why   does   your   heart

start   beating   when   you

read   your   poems ?

love   from
Mrs Duffy

Example 2e

Dear   mrs   Duffy
My   heart Starts
beating when I read
my poems It makes me
wobeleare   very   very
Very   very   very
very very   Very
mouts
Lots   of
love From
Aileen
x x

Example 2f

By luck rather than judgment something really interested Aileen.
Suddenly the voice changed from a fairly staid quality to a highly
individual response. It is as if Aileen had suddenly come alive. This sense
of dynamism once gained was not lost.

Dear Aileen

I like your pony tail and your new pinafore . Have you seen the broken window in our classroom ? What do you think happened ?

love from

Mrs Duffy

Example 3a

Dear mrs Duffy I got my now pinafore from marks and sheners I wonted to have it my mummy give i't to me I have seen the window I thik it wos a boy he trow a brik

thank you very

mots

lots of

Love from

Aileen

Example 3b

Dear   Aileen

Where   has   your   pony
tail   gone   today ?
Perhaps   a   boy   threw   a
stone .   I   found   a   golf ball
on   the   floor .   I   wonder
where   it   came   from ?

love   from

Mrs Duffy

Example 3c

Dear   mrs   Duffy my
Mum   tuk   my pony
tail   out I think the
golf   ball   broken   the
Window

Lots

Of   love

from

Aileen

Example 3d

The exchanges have now moved from the simple one question one
answer to the holding of two elements of content. Aileen has
demonstrated that she is capable of handling more than one topic in a
letter. Could she have done this all the time I wondered or was it
something thing she had just learned to do? Aileen's responses were,

however, still responses to my questions. She has not really moved beyond a typical teacher/child oral language relationship. In an attempt to initiate this shift I decided to try a different tack. I would invite her to ask me something.

Dear Aileen

I know lots of things about you. Would you like to ask me any questions?

love from

Mrs Duffy

xxx

Example 4a

Dear Mrs Duffy Denny is coming todey and Sined and Kevin magline are coming afear dinner

lots of love from Aileen

Example 4b

In other words 'no', Aileen would not like to ask me any questions. However, it has led to a shift. For the first time Aileen has moved from responding to a question to generating a novel topic. Perhaps it was desperation at finding herself expected to make some kind of contribution.

Dear Aileen

Who are Sinead and

Kevin? Why are they

coming after dinner?

love from

Mrs Duffy.

Example 5a

Dear mrs Duffy Sinneud
is my coson and kevin
is my coson and Denny
is my brother Lucy is
my frerred

Lots of love

Aileen

Example 5b

I still wanted to try and get a genuine dialogue; one in which both parties functioned equally. The strategy I decided upon was to stop asking questions (a difficult strategy for a teacher) and simply introduce topics for comment.

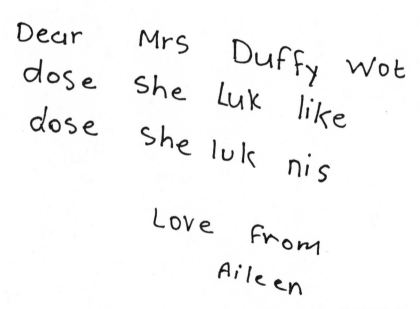

Dear   Aileen

I have   a   friend

called   Judy.

                    Love   from

                    Mrs Duffy

Example 6a

Dear   Mrs   Duffy wot
dose   she   luk like
dose   she luk nis

            Love from
                Aileen

Example 6b

Hey presto! Aileen's first question. She has moved from respondent to questioner. From this moment on the exchange moves to quite a different level, a level of friendship and interest that is, in my experience, extremely rare in a teacher/child written dialogue. However, in order for that to be the case I had to be prepared to offer information about myself. Morally one cannot expect children to expose feelings, beliefs, and personal histories unless one is going to do so as well.

Dear   Aileen

She   is   very   tall   and   very
pretty.   . She   has   blonde   hair.
She   is   kind   and   makes
me   laugh.

love   from
Mrs   Duffy

Example 7a

Dear   mrS   Duffy   I
like   blonde   hair
My   dols   got   blonde   hair
is   She   bigr   an   mistr
greed   is   She   very   very
kind   and   loveley

Lots   of love from
Aileen   PS.   thank

you

Example 7b

Suddenly a 'PS'. Where does this come from? Later when Aileen was asked where she had learned about a PS, she said she had seen her elder brother use one.

Dear   Aileen
She   is   bigger   than   I
am   but   not   as   big   as
Mr   Greenall.   She   is
very   kind   and   makes
me   laugh.   I went   to
her   house   last   night.

love   from   Mrs   Duffy

p.s.   I   liked   your   letter

Example 8a

Dear mrs Duffy wot
time did you go at
dici you tae ps
I wad like a
notr letter

Example 8b

Dear Aileen, It was
7 o'clock when I arrived.
I had fish fingers and
chips for tea. I could not
go earlier because I was
upset.
        Love from
            Mrs Duffy
p.s. I enjoyed my tea
very much

Example 8c

Dear   mrs   DUffy   I   go
to bed at 7 o'clock   way
Wor   you   upset
          ps   I hop you
had   a   nis   time

          Love from
               Aileen

Example 8d

Dear   Aileen   I had a
lovely time   thank you
but   I   was   worried about
Tess   my   dog.   She is
sick.
          Love   from
               Mrs Duffy

Example 8e

Dear Mrs Duffy I now
you love   your dog
   do you kis him and
   pat   him or enyting
like that   love from
          Ailcen

Example 8f

Dear Aileen, she is a lovely dog. When my feet are cold she lies on them to make them warm .

love from

Mrs Duffy

Example 8g

Dear Mr Duffy She is verey verey loveley is yur feet verey verey cold wen She lies on them Wen my feet are cold I put them in a bol of hot watr they sun get verey verey warm

love from
Aileen

Example 8h

Conclusion

The term came to an end and as it was the summer term the exchange ceased. Even though the dialogue lasted only a short time, it seemed that the introduction of dialogue journals led, in this instance, to some quite dramatic changes in the style, quality, and interest of Aileen's authorship. It also changed some of my authorship; I think I developed a more relaxed style with Aileen that enabled a more sincere relationship to develop. Through the way I handled the dialogue I was offering a demonstration about how words can be used to explore personal relationships and by responding to what Aileen wrote in a totally sincere way I was accepting Aileen as a fully literate person. Thus, in this exchange there were demonstrations, opportunities, and acceptance. These combine to give this kind of authorship a very high status. It was a wonderful way to facilitate the continued emergence of literacy.

Aileen had discovered her inner voice as a result of communication to a real audience, someone who was not standing over her shoulder as she wrote, and someone who she knew would be interested in what she had to say and would treat her words with respect. It was evident that she was enjoying this discovery very much. When her writing was compared with the previous cloned efforts, a number of points were evident. Aileen now seemed to write with much more purpose, and her efforts were no longer stilted and laboured. She wrote quickly and animatedly and, freed from spelling restrictions, her vocabulary had improved. She no longer used only safe words from the basal reader and was now conscious of a real audience. As a result, her confidence grew and the sense of 'self' in her writing was gradually emerging.

I suspect, however, that the reason it was emerging was less to do with Aileen now knowing how to do it, but rather her having the freedom to actually do it. I will never know whether Aileen could have written like this a long time before she did; I never gave her the opportunity to show me that she could. By emphasising correct spelling and neat handwriting I may have forced her, and all the other children, into a conservative stance on writing. A stance that limited their opportunities to grow as authors and communicators. The authorship of all the children was now quite distinctive. There was no way anyone could accuse the children of writing in a 'cloned' fashion. The children were no longer restricted by the need to feel secure. Their security was now within the freedom to express, in their own way, those things which appealed to, or interested, them most.

A written dialogue with one's class teacher is perhaps a limited kind of audience for young children and there are undoubtedly many other audiences that could have been used. However, it certainly worked with these particular children and has worked with classes since. The children seemed to appreciate the sense of mystery that comes from writing to a reader who is not present at the time of writing; they wonder what the reaction will be and what will be the reply. It also seemed to lead to a closer relationship with the children. They enjoyed the sense of a special relationship with their teacher.

—5— Writing Rules – OK

Jill Pauling

Introduction

It was a project on dinosaurs that first caused me to stand back and wonder. I had carefully planned and prepared flow-diagrams and collected resources; I had a pretty good idea of the direction that the topic would take. I thought that three or four species, correctly named, would be all that my five-year-olds would be able to cope with.

After two days I realised that, despite two-thirds of the class coming from homes where English was not the only language spoken, these five-year-olds were not going to be satisfied with the level of factual information that I had been able to provide. They produced books, in several languages, containing pictures and text about dinosaurs that I had never heard of. Together we struggled to read the names of no less than thirty-one giant lizards.

By this time the topic had generated a life of its own and a small group became fascinated by fossils, and paleontology in general. Various plant and simple animal fossils were brought into school. Discussion focused on the storing and display of this collection. Interest then spread to the idea of museums and the group, which now numbered six children, decided to create a museum in the classroom activity area. Having established the museum they decided that some of the exhibits were too precious to allow haphazard handling. They began to work on a set of rules for the museum. A first draft was generated and subsequently a published set of rules appeared which, they hoped, would govern behaviour in their museum. Their document read:

A list of rules you have to follow when you visit a museum.

1 Be quiet.
2 Don't touch.
3 Do not steal anything.
4 Do not litter inside the museum.
5 Draw the pictures of the things inside the museum.
6 Take one leaflet from the museum when you leave the place.
7 Don't forget to buy postcards.

The rules were read to the rest of the class and clauses like '7' were explained and discussed. It appeared that the 'leaflet' would include information as to what to do should you find a dinosaur fossil in the playground at school, and what a paleontologist could do to help. I was amazed at the high level of thinking which had underpinned the development of the rules.

Listening to their explanations I began to realise the extent to which even the youngest children had been able to discuss and negotiate in order to shape the work of the group. Left to themselves, they had gradually developed and refined their ideas. They appeared perfectly capable of constructing a carefully reasoned set of rules to control other people's behaviour. It seemed that the very act of composing rules had generated a learning environment in which written information was refined and processed by discussion.

Dial 999: the police cells

Our next project was called 'Dial 999'. The first part of this involved the Hong Kong Police Force. We made contact with parents who were policemen and collected information pamphlets, reference books, and commercial posters. The activity area of the classroom was turned into a police station, complete with command centre, reporting desk, switchboard and lock-up cell. Initially, the play took the form of policemen capturing robbers and putting them in the police cell. When several inmates were left there for any length of time havoc ensued and I found myself having to intervene as an arbitrator. I had been looking for an opportunity to return to 'rule writing' and this situation seemed to offer an appropriate opportunity. I suggested that they might like to draw up a set of rules to govern behaviour within the lock-up cell. A group of five children sat down to discuss the problem.

As a consequence of the previous rule writing, I had determined that if children wrote rules again, I wanted to know what they talked about. My presence would, inevitably, have hindered their conversation and the obvious solution (although not a perfect one) was to record their talk. The children agreed to let me do this.

I distanced myself from the group but, even from afar, it was obvious that discussion was intense. Of the five children involved, four speak two languages (Shohei still finds it a struggle to express himself fully in English) and Gavin is a native English speaker.

1	*Yi-Sheng*:	Of course we may not need any rules.
2	*Shelley*:	We ought to make them just in case.
3	*Yi-Sheng*:	We ought not let any children in the jail and . . .
4	*Gavin*:	We should say 'No children in the jail' then.
5	*Shohei*:	Make sure the walls are strong.
6	*Nhishanth*:	Yes . . . make sure the walls are strong . . . I'll check them.
7	*Shelly*:	No . . . we're making rules now.
8	*Shohei*:	'No lights' . . . well lights are dangerous.
9	*Gavin*:	Well . . . no light bulbs, but the robbers could use light bulbs to break things.
10	*Yi-Sheng*:	I know . . . 'No cigarettes'.

11	*Shohei*:	That's good because they might burn holes in things.
12	*Yi-Sheng*:	Anyway I must say, my grandma died of cancer.
13	*Shohei*:	I know cancer.
14	*Yi-Sheng*:	So let's put 'No cigarettes'.
15	*Shelley*:	(*Spells out*) 'N o c i g a r e t t e s'.
16	*Gavin*:	'No guns' . . . no real guns. Your dad might have a real gun and he was holding it like this and showing it to the robbers and the robbers might snatch it and he might cheat you.
17	*Yi-Sheng*:	OK so no real guns . . . good idea Gavin.
18	*Shohei*:	'Only one robber in the cell at a time' . . . because maybe they would make power if there was two and escape and break the lock.
19	*Gavn*:	And they would make plans to escape.
20	*Yi-Sheng*:	You wouldn't give them a real gun, I know, but if you did you could look and see there were no real bullets inside.
21	*Shohei*:	But a robber might have some already . . . so no real guns.
22	*Gavin*:	What about 'No belts' as they could use them to whip people.
23	*Yi-Sheng*:	OK . . . no belts.
24	*Gavin*:	'No matches or caps'.
25	*Shelley*:	I'll put 'No matches'.
26	*Shohei*:	'No pencils' . . . sharpened pencils because they could be a weapon. I know . . . 'No bombs'.
27	*Yi-Sheng*:	Are prisoners allowed to eat?
28	*Gavin*:	Only one time a day.
29	*Yi-Sheng*:	I don't think they would give the prisoners dessert.
30	*Gavin*:	'No ice-cream or desserts for the robbers' because the robbers might lift up the ice-cream and when the policeman comes, he could throw it.
31	*Shohei*:	And then they can escape.
32	*Shelley*:	You've written 'ices'.
33	*Yi-Sheng*:	Yes, that's short for ice-cream.
34	*Nhishanth*:	You can write that.
35	*Shohei*:	(*Writing*) 'No real guns'.
36	*Gavin*:	He's up to 'guns' . . . 'No light bulbs', because he might take it off you and break it and use it as a weapon.
37	*Yi-Sheng*:	'No glass at all' . . . I haven't got any more room on my paper.
38	*Shohei*:	I can't seem to spell electric.
39	*Gavin*:	Eee lll ectric.
40	*Yi-Sheng*:	I guess there's another reason for no desserts.
41	*Shohei*:	I know one, because maybe he can use it as a trick to make the policeman not look at . . .
42	*Yi-Sheng*:	Yes he pretends he has got a stomach ache and goes to tell the medical room and the policeman might leave the keys behind and the robber might take the keys and unlock himself.
43	*Gavin*:	They won't have meat.

44	*Shohei*:	Yes, because they might use the bones as weapons.
45	*Gavin*:	There's another reason for not using meat . . . because it makes them strong.
46	*Yi-Sheng*:	They wouldn't survive without meat actually, so they could give them bones without meat.
47	*Nhishanth*:	Vegetarians don't eat meat.
48	*Yi-Sheng*:	They eat fish and fish is meat.
49	*Shelley*:	Some eat eggs . . . are eggs meat?
50	*Yi-Sheng*:	Yes . . . No . . . I don't know . . . anyway they couldn't use egg shells as weapons. If they only had egg it would be very messy. Plates can be broken and he can cut his hands loose if they were tied together.
51	*Shohei*:	You can't use metal plates because he might take it off you and hurt you.
52	*Shelley*:	So what about paper or plastic plates?
53	*Shohei*:	Plastic is best.

This extract from the transcript reveals clearly that for these children composition is an intellectual process. The activity of generating their draft texts has them involved in an exchange of ideas about a wide range of adult behaviour and values.

To begin with they establish the need for such a task and as the discussion continues so the individual roles are generated and maintained. Yi-Sheng seems to initially assume leadership (1, 14, 17). In these three turns he considers the credibility of the task, directs the group to putting something down on paper, and offers affirmation to another in the group. Shelley, although relatively quiet, operates to bring the group's focus back to the nature of the task (2, 7, and 32). Shohei and Gavin seem to be the principal idea generators and are constantly adding new dimensions to the collaborative composition (8, 9, 16, 18, 22, 26, 30, 43, 44), although Yi-Sheng is also an active contributor. Nhishanth takes on the role of scribe, which may account for the relatively small number of contributions he makes to the discussion.

The children draw on knowledge, personal experience and imagination in drawing up their rules. Yi-Sheng introduces the subject of smoking and has obviously been affected by his grandmother's recent death from cancer (12 and see next transcript). For the other children cigarettes are simply a potential source of burning. The subject of guns (16, 17, 20, 21) and other likely weapons generates some perceptive thinking as a variety of sharp, incendiary, or explosive articles are eliminated. The issue of whether or not 'robbers' should be fed in jail offers a chance for some very creative reasoning (27–52). Having decided that desserts could be used to divert policemen, they decide that meat bones could also be deployed as weapons.

In this extract of transcript we see exchange, debate, and development. The rules which result are not just an arbitrary list; they are the product of careful thought. The rules at this stage though are still in draft form as the bell sounded and the session came to an end.

Three of the group met later to redraft their rules for publication. The finished set of rules was to be placed on the front of the police cell. The three found it much harder to work in a smaller group and there was quite a lot of recapping previous conversation. However, this recapping solidified the reasoning that lay behind the published set of rules. The transcript makes clear that all decisions about the organisation of the text were being made by the children themselves.

1	*Yi-Sheng*:	Let's try and remember the rules we started to make the other day . . . 'No desserts'.
2	*Nhishanth*:	'No guns'.
3	*Shohei*:	'No shoelaces' . . . they can be used for tying around your neck.
4	*Yi-Sheng*:	Actually don't forget what Miss Taylor said about school uniform being extremely safe.
5	*Nhishanth*:	'No smoking.'
6	*Yi-Sheng*:	Listen . . . there is . . . there are ties and ties are like string.
7	*Nhishanth*:	'No desserts.'
8	*Shohei*:	'No meat' . . . no meat in bones.
9	*Yi-Sheng*:	No . . . no bones in the meat no meat in the bones.
10	*Shohei*:	'No guns or bombs' . . . it says 'No bombs' over there.
11	*Nhishanth*:	'Always keep the keys hidden far away.'
12	*Yi-Sheng*:	Yes and 'Do not tell where the keys are'.
13	*Nhishanth*:	And 'Do not have the telephone near the cells'.
14	*Yi-Sheng*:	Nhishanth, if you write that hard you might break your wrist or break the pencil.
15	*Nhishanth*:	'No children in the cells.'
16	*Shohei*:	'Only one robber at a time in the cells.'
17	*Yi-Sheng*:	Let's start writing on the big sheet now.
18	*Shohei*:	Can you start writing with . . . 'No guns or bombs'?
19	*Nhishanth*:	Is that the most important?
20	*Yi-Sheng*:	I think 'No sweets' would be good but we should have 'No sweets or bubble gum'.
21	*Nhishanth*:	'No children' I think that is important.
22	*Yi-Sheng*:	I guess we should start with what Shohei said . . . 'No guns or bombs' . . . rule number 1 . . . go ahead, you write the first bit Nhishanth and I'll write the 'because' bit.
23	*Shohei*:	Maybe the next one is 'No shoelaces or ties' because that could kill you too.
24	*Yi-Sheng*:	Give us more time to write please.
25	*Nhishanth*:	(*Slowly*) 'No guns or bombs because bombs can explode and guns can shoot bullets.'
26	*Yi-Sheng*:	OK . . . rule number 2.
27	*Shohei*:	What was it?
28	*Yi-Sheng*:	'No shoelaces or ties.'
29	*Shohei*:	Let's check what we did . . . I'll cross them off the list.
30	*Nhishanth*:	Which one Shohei? Choose us one . . . remember Yi-Sheng you write the words after 'because'.
31	*Shohei*:	I crossed off the ones we did.
32	*Yi-Sheng*:	I finished that . . . choose another one Shohei.
33	*Shohei*:	Let's choose this . . . 'Always keep the keys hidden and

far away'.

34	*Nhishanth*:	Oops I forgot something.
35	*Shohei*:	Here you forgot to put 'Rule number 3'.
36	*Yi-Sheng*:	Can I have the pencil after you?
37	*Nhishanth*:	Sure.
38	*Shohei*:	What is next?
39	*Nishanth*:	Hey Yi-Sheng . . . leave that book alone. I've put 'Always keep keys out of reach' . . . it's your turn now.
40	*Shohei*:	Where are you up to?
41	*Nhishanth*:	I'm here and I want you to do this. (*Long pause filled by silent writing activity.*) Have you finished with it?
42	*Shohei*:	OK . . . next one . . . now it's 'No meat because of bones'.
43	*Nhishanth*:	Look I didn't write the proper sentence that you said . . . I wrote another one but they mean the same thing . . . right?
44	*Shohei*:	'Rule number 5' . . . I think I will write 'No desserts'.
45	*Yi-Sheng*:	No first write 'No meat because of the bones'.
46	*Nhishanth*:	(*Writing*) 'No meat with bones because'. . . no it's his turn . . . write 'Because they can use them as weapons'.
47	*Shohei*:	Now let's write 'No desserts' . . . come on I've counted there's one, two, three more to do.
48	*Nhishanth*:	What did you say?
49	*Shohei*:	I said 'No desserts' . . . did you write it?
50	*Yi-Sheng*:	Do we have the one about the telephones?
51	*Nhishanth*:	I'll help Yi-Sheng with the desserts because he has the toughest job writing in the 'becauses'.
52	*Shohei*:	OK Yi-Sheng . . . 'because he might throw it at you'.
53	*Nhishanth*:	Hey you forgot to write in the word 'because'.
54	*Shohei*:	Ai ee you can't do that . . . have you got a rubber?
55	*Yi-Sheng*:	'Because they might throw it at you or' . . . I wish Shelley was here . . . she was missing yesterday and missing today.
56	*Shohei*:	They might pretend to have tummy ache and go to the medical room.
57	*Yi-Sheng*:	I think I'll change that last one to 'and trick the cops'.
58	*Nhishanth*:	What's a cop?
59	*Shohei*:	Policeman of course.
60	*Yi-Sheng*:	Can you put 'No children in the cells'?
61	*Nhishanth*:	OK rule number 6 . . . it should be the one about the sweets first.
62	*Yi-Sheng*:	I think you should put bubble gum because some sweets like bubble gum are sticky . . .
63	*Nhishanth*:	Sticky and they might stick on your shoes . . .
64	*Yi-Sheng*:	And a robber might put it out of the cell and the policeman might step on it.
65	*Shohei*:	Then maybe they could get out because sometimes when it's lunchtime and he carefully spitted it out on the ground, then the policeman steps on it . . . he opens the door and steps on it and they . . .
66	*Yi-Sheng*:	Shhhhhh

67	*Shohei*:	. . . Then maybe the thief gets out.
68	*Yi-Sheng*:	Rubber . . . Rubber . . . Rubber . . .
69	*Shohei*:	(*Beginning to lose interest because the scribes are not able to keep up with his flow of ideas and are becoming impatient with him*) What's the time?
70	*Yi-Sheng*:	Ai Yee . . . that writing is too big!
71	*Nhishanth*:	No . . . it's too slanted.
72	*Shohei*:	Now I remember . . . 'No children in the cells'.
73	*Yi-Sheng*:	Actually cells are also part of the body.
74	*Nhishanth*:	Yi-Sheng?
75	*Yi-Sheng*:	Yes.
76	*Nishanth*:	Why did you make that rule?
77	*Yi-Sheng*:	Because the thief might trick the children.
78	*Shohei*:	Maybe the children is one of the thief's friends . . . maybe?
79	*Nhishanth*:	Do we need to stick rules everywhere? Can we get a photocopy?
80	*Shohei*:	OK what now?
81	*Nhishanth*:	What's rule number 8?
82	*Shohei*:	(*Checking his rough draft*) 'Only one robber at a time'.
83	*Yi-Sheng*:	Yes . . . because they might help each other.
84	*Nhishanth*:	The 'No smoking' rule is the longest one here.
85	*Shohei*:	I didn't know it was . . . 'do not smoke because you might get lung cancer or the robbers could use the cigarette to burn the rope'.
86	*Nhishanth*:	Wait a minute . . . just wait a minute.
87	*Yi-Sheng*:	'Rule number 9' . . . 'No smoking because . . .'
88	*Shohei*:	Can we . . . when we always . . . can we have . . . can we die sometime when you always work hard and don't stop?
89	*Nhishanth*:	You won't die . . . no.
90	*Shohei*:	Well my mummy's daddy did.
91	*Nhishanth*:	Does he work too hard do you mean?
92	*Shohei*:	Yes . . . I know I mean . . .
93	*Yi-Sheng*:	It's not like smoking . . . we must put 'No smoking' here because you might . . .
94	*Nhishanth*:	Have you crossed 'No smoking' out?
95	*Shohei*:	It's too long . . . I'll just cross out 'No smoke'.
96	*Yi-Sheng*:	How do you spell 'nicotine'?
97	*Nhishanth*:	N I C O N T E E N
98	*Yi-Sheng*:	My father said that the Indians invented cigarettes . . . I'm going to put cigars not cigarettes . . . they are the same thing . . . (muttering) cancer can cause death.
99	*Nhishanth*:	They also could use it to burn the door down.
100	*Yi-Sheng*:	OK that's it now . . . I've finished . . . let's put it up.

I was interested to note the strategies the children used and the ways in which they organised themselves, for the redrafting of the set of rules, and how they worked out an order of priority for writing the final draft. After Yi-Sheng's initial invitation to remember all the important things from the first discussion, the whole group contributes a variety of suggestions. Again Yi-Sheng (1, 17, 22) emerges to take the role of leader and brings the group together to start writing. They decide that two of them will act as scribes and Shohei has to read from the first draft and amend the ideas for the final publication (29–31 and see Example 1).

Shohei used the previous drafts to monitor that all points were recalled

2 no meat becase bones are good weapons.
3 only paper or plastic plates.
4 the key should be hidden
5 put the telephone far from the jail room

L only one person in charge or in the cel
2 no children in the jail room
3 no cigarites
4 no real guns
5 no belts berties because he might whip
6 no matches or sweet or use
7 no deserts or ices because he might throw it at you

Example 1

All parties make a surprising effort not to get exasperated when the flow of ideas is too fast for the writers, and several entries illustrate the degree of cooperation between the children with regard to the organisation of the writing (29–41). Cooperation was certainly needed as a result of the decision that one of them should write the rule and the other should write the explanation. On several occasions the person doing the writing changes the suggested text. Nhishanth (43) paraphrases Shohei's sentence and Yi–Sheng (56) decides to introduce the word 'cop'. For once Nhishanth is caught out and questions the meaning, and thus new information is shared by the group. Another good illustration of this is when Yi–Sheng remembers an alternative meaning for the word 'cell' (73), and offers this information to the group. The relationship between smoking and lung cancer gives rise to further interesting talk, in particular Yi–Sheng's information that his father told him that Indians invented cigarettes. In the resulting discussion it is clear that Shohei is bothered by his grandfather's death from overwork and he tries to check with the group whether he too will die if he works too hard. Fortunately, the general feeling is that Shohei will not die. However, further discussion is terminated by Yi–Sheng's announcement that the rules are finished. These rules (see Example 2) were placed in the police cell and were the focus of much lively discussion for several weeks.

Our project then moved on to look at the hospital service and the activity area was once again transformed, this time from a police cell into a hospital. At this point, many questions were asked about road accidents and first aid. It seemed an ideal opportunity to look at the way the rule-making process could be adapted for devising a set of instructions to give to ambulance crews as they set off to answer a '999' call. A group of six children wanted to work on a draft and the following transcript demonstrates some of the ways in which they went about it. Again, the children were all five- or six-years-old and the information that was brought to bear on the task was, for the most part, not information that they had been taught in school.

1	*Tom*:	All right then, what instructions shall we give to the ambulance driver?
2	*Nhishanth*:	The first thing is knowing where to go.
3	*Gavin*:	Well . . . you should ask them where it is . . . like is it a Quarry Bay School somewhere?
4	*Sally*:	You get a map and there are words that tell you what a place it is and you find out where it is.
5	*Jenny*:	And when you get to the accident you know because you can see everyone gathered around.
6	*Gavin*:	To keep the crowds away . . . you'd get a long chain . . .
7	*Jenny*:	And put a circle around them and . . .
8	*Gavin*:	Well . . . the ambulance men would get out and get the person who was bad . . . really bad and put them on the trailer which is like . . . well it straps on you.
9	*Nhishanth*:	A stretcher.
10	*Gavin*:	Yes a stretcher and they pull it into the ambulance and drive off.
11	*Sally*:	You could keep the crowds . . . you could get a rope and tie it onto the side of a bar and if some girls pass by . . . they can tell them to keep back.
12	*Gavin*:	You've got to keep back the crowds you know because when someone crosses the road they might step on the injured person.

The published rules as written by Yi-Sheng and Nhishanth

Rules of Behaviour in the cell at the police station

Rule no 1

No guns or Bombs : Because Bombs can explode and guns can shoot (with bullits)

Rule No 2

No shoelaces and ties be cause you can tie other people with it

Rule no. 3

Always keep the key out of reach because the theif might reach it.

Rule No 4

No meat with bones because they can use them as weapons

Rule no 5

No deserts because they might throw it at you. They could also pretend to have a tummy ache and trick the cop

Rule no 6

No sweets an Bubble gum : because he might step on it afther the theif puts it on the ground

Rule no. 7

No children in the cells : because the theif might trick him/her and get out.

Rule No. 8

Only one theif at a time : because they might help each other

Rule No. nine 9.

No smokeing : because cigars have nicoteen in them and nicoteen can cause canser and canser can cause death. They also could use it to burn the door down.

Example 2

13	*Nhishanth*:	You've got to see if one is breathing . . . say one of them isn't breathing?
14	*Jenny*:	You blow into their mouths.
15	*Nhishanth*:	What?
16	*Gavin*:	Yes . . . you blow into their mouths.
17	*Tom*:	No you put a special bag that is full of air and you've got this sort of pipe . . . I think you have to put it in your mouth but I don't know . . . and there's a short pump and you blow all the air in.
18	*Nhishanth*:	I'll make a note of that . . . Number 3.
19	*Gavin*:	You can blow in their mouths.
20	*Jenny*:	They must also see if their heart's not beating.
21	*Gavin*:	If it's not beating . . . you have to hammer on them . . . on here.
22	*Tom*:	You mean on their chest.
23	*Gavin*:	Then you've got to see if they've got broken arms. You can tell . . . if they say 'ow' then it's broken . . . you can move it a little bit and if they say 'ow' you better not do it . . . then you know.
24	*Tom*:	What about if they're unconscious?
25	*Jenny*:	What does it mean 'unconscious'?
26	*Nhishanth*:	It means you don't know anything around you.
27	*Gavin*:	Then you sort of show them around and you have to help them know where everything is.
28	*Sally*:	If you see their mum or dad you can give them to their mum or dad.
29	*Jenny*:	You've got to keep people warm.
30	*Christine*:	No . . . hot like a very hot bath would be good.
31	*Nhishanth*:	Yes . . . a very hot one but you couldn't do that at the ambulance.
32	*Gavin*:	But you could give them a blanket.
33	*Jenny*:	You've got to stop people saying 'You're going to die soon'.
34	*Gavin*:	Because it would frighten them and they would ask the ambulance man if they would die.
35	*Jenny*:	And they might cry.
36	*Gavin*:	Then you'd give them a nice ice-lolly.

It was clear from the outset that the children had grasped the difference between 'rules' and 'instructions', and their approach was less didactic than before. The suggestions were mainly positive, in contrast to the list of negative rules devised for the police cell.

An important point is raised in the discussion about unconsciousness which highlights the misconceptions that many children have about the meanings of words. Tom has raised the subject of unconsciousness and the children begin to explore the meaning of the word. Gavin has heard, some time in the past, someone talk about 'bringing an unconscious person around' and in his mind he equates this with showing someone around. The group are generally agreed that accident victims must be kept warm but various suggestions are rejected by the group as impractical (30). Jenny introduces the notion of preventing onlookers from telling the accident victims that they are going to die, and this is instantly accepted by Gavin who suggests a way of cheering up the victim (36). His suggestion is, like his earlier point about unconsciousness, a delightful demonstration of how young children desperately, and sensibly, attempt to render experiences meaningful.

The generation of their draft texts is, once again, not simply a process of adding, incrementally, bits to a list. When suggestions are made they are responded to, frequently amended and developed, in some way. The development of the text is an interactive process and the text is much more powerful as a result. Their draft texts may not, self-evidently, reflect the depth of thinking that underpins them; the transcript though reveals it all. It is a clear signal to teachers that judgments about the intellectual quality of children's writing require more than just a text. During this session some of the children had been writing up drafts of the instructions (see Example 3).

Tom and Sally's draft versions of the ambulancemen's instructions

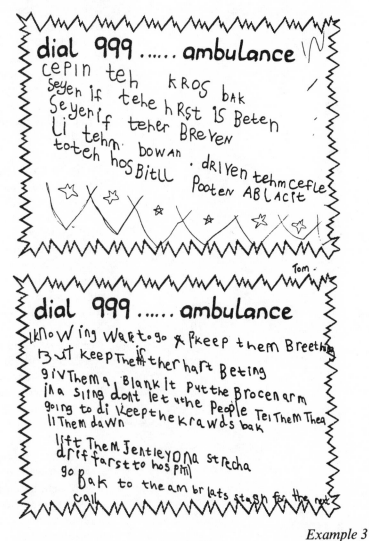

Example 3

When the children met again the group had changed with Yi-Sheng and Shohei deciding to join in. They had in front of them the draft versions and they were trying to establish the format for the set of instructions they would publish for the class. Nhishanth is chosen as the scribe, although they previously decided that once this final draft was made it would be word-processed so that several copies could be printed and displayed.

1	*Yi-Sheng*:	OK now we've got to look at these and make a proper set of rules . . . are there any more pieces of paper? . . . you write Nhishanth.
2	*Nhishanth*:	Now what do we need first?
3	*Yi-Sheng*:	Keeping back the crowds . . . now let me see . . . 'Keeping back the crowds' must be number 1.
4	*Jenny*:	Knowing where to go . . . isn't 'Knowing where to go' . . . isn't that first?
5	*Yi-Sheng*:	I think you're right . . . hi Gavin.
6	*Gavin*:	Sorry I'm late.
7	*Shohei*:	We were waiting for you.
8	*Gavin*:	What are you doing?
9	*Jenny*:	Writing the instructions . . . '1' is 'Knowing where to go' . . . the ambulance men have to know you see because . . .
10	*Shohei*:	They might get lost or pick up the wrong people.
11	*Yi-Sheng*:	OK number 2 . . . 'Keep out the crowd' . . . that means keep it back.
12	*Jenny*:	'Make sure they are breathing' . . . that's just as important as keeping the crowds back.
13	*Gavin*:	If they are breathing you can say they are OK.
14	*Jenny*:	If they are not breathing they might die.
15	*Shohei*:	But you've got to stop them bleeding . . . if you don't they will die . . . I knowed.
16	*Sally*:	How much bleeding can they do?
17	*Yi-Sheng*:	You have about 4 pints of blood . . . I think . . . when you're this age . . . I read it.
18	*Shohei*:	So how much could you lose and not die?
19	*Gavin*:	Nearly all of it . . . well no not 100 per cent.
20	*Tom*:	I reckon if you lost about most of it you'd have 1 per cent more and you might die.
21	*Gavin*:	I reckon it is about 10 per cent.
22	*Nhishanth*:	What do I write next? I've got first . . . I've done 1, 2, and 3 . . . but is there any more about crowds?
23	*Yi-Sheng*:	I don't think they want to be bothered by that . . . well by lots of crowds I mean.
24	*Gavin*:	Because they might spread germs and the crowds might disturb the ambulance men.
25	*Nhishanth*:	'Keep them breathing' . . . go on we've got to there now . . . see I've written 'Keep them breathing'.
26	*Shohei*:	Supposing they're not . . . how do you know if they were breathing?
27	*Tom*:	You do this (*pushes his chest in and out*).

28	*Jenny*:	You look here (*indicates chest*).
29	*Gavin*:	And you give them this special oxygen.
30	*Tom*:	And there is this little bag and it's full of air and you put all the air into their mouth and then all the germs come out and then they can breathe.
31	*Sally*:	You've got to tell about their heart beating.
32	*Gavin*:	Yes or otherwise they'll die . . . you can see it it's working because they move.
33	*Jenny*:	You bang them if they don't but you have to get special training to do that.
34	*Tom*:	You have to get a pulse.
35	*Shohei*:	What's that?
36	*Tom*:	Its a bone here (*points to his wrist*) if the bone isn't there you die.
37	*Nishanth*:	The next one is about blankets . . . shall I put about blankets?
38	*Jenny*:	Yes because if they are cold they might freeze and the blood might come out more.
39	*Tom*:	If someone's been crashed over they might need a blanket to keep them not so ill.
40	*Sally*:	Is it called shock . . . it's called shock . . . I heard it . . . I got shock.
41	*Shohei*:	You got shock?
42	*Sally*:	I touched this electric wire and it felt bad.
43	*Gavin*:	I got a shock with an electric hairdryer . . . you can you know.
44	*Yi-Sheng*:	You get nervous.
45	*Nhishanth*:	What's next . . . do I put about broken arms?
46	*Gavin*:	No just get to the hospital otherwise they might die fast.
47	*Jenny*:	Or be sick.
48	*Shohei*:	If you go fast . . .
49	*Yi-Sheng*:	I can't hear you Shohei . . .
50	*Shohei*:	If you go too fast you could make it worse and they could die.
51	*Tom*:	You have to lift them on a stretcher . . . you could put a strap around them but gently . . . you've got to go gently or you could be badder for them.
52	*Gavin*:	He's trying to say that . . . we'll get them to hospital . . . take a short cut fast . . . fast without stopping.
53	*Shohei*:	Without hurting the person . . . use a stretcher.
54	*Gavin*:	Strap them really tight . . . so then if there's another accident the patient could be worse.
55	*Tom*:	Yes if the door is unlocked it might get open and the passenger fall out and they wouldn't know when they got to hospital where it had gone and if another car was coming then they might get another road accident and die straight away.
56	*Nhishanth*:	Shall I put 'Give them drinks' . . . shall we say some . . . a little . . . drink if they're thirsty.
57	*Gavin*:	Give them special drinks.

58	*Jenny:*	No . . . if you have an operation you could feel sick . . . when I had my tonsils out last week I didn't get a drink . . . not before anyway.
59	*Tom:*	My granny couldn't have a drink because she had to have an operation for her stomach ache.
60	*Gavin:*	You might get the wrong stuff.
61	*Shohei:*	It might make you sick.
62	*Yi-Sheng:*	I think they will have to put labels anyway . . . you couldn't survive without water . . . you can't live without water or food.
63	*Shohei:*	Does everyone who has a road accident have to have an operation?
64	*Tom:*	Yes . . . well if it was a bad wound . . . they would have to check it to see if . . . say there was two broken legs . . . they'd have to check it and open the legs . . . they have to check it and open the legs and if they found two broken legs . . . they'd have to sew them up and put them in plaster.
65	*Gavin:*	No you don't have to do that . . . there's a strong light . . . an X-ray . . . and this picture which . . . well the light goes on and then the pictures there . . . like that . . . and the light shows right in.
66	*Nhishanth:*	Before you say about that . . . how about after 'Don't give too much drinks' . . . how about 'Call the police' and leave it to them . . . you could make the cars stop and make the road clear . . . but the best is to dial 999 and get the police.
67	*Tom:*	That's good and then go back to the ambulance station and warm up . . . yes warm up and wait for the next call.
68	*Yi-Sheng:*	Can you write that Nhishanth . . . can you remember that?
69	*Nhishanth:*	I nearly finished . . . Shohei . . . you did some writing too.

The group start to compile the list when Gavin rejoins them. They automatically recap so that he can take part in the activity. When they get to Shohei's comment (15) about bleeding, an interesting conversation arises about how much blood a person could lose and yet still survive. Yi-Sheng refers to 'four pints' and yet at school he has only ever learned metric capacity. Gavin and Tom (19–21) talk about percentages in an apparently accurate way, yet again they have never been taught the word or the concept at school; they are only five and six! Tom (30) adds another dimension to his thinking about the oxygen mask, with his comment about 'germs coming out' which he feels will somehow enable the patient to breath. Jenny now gives a cautionary warning about heart massage (33) and has found out that you should only do it if you have been trained. It is remarkable how much thinking (or perhaps asking) has gone on between the two sessions. Sally now seems to know why a patient must be kept warm and her question about shock again reflects the enduring quest to puzzle out the confusions caused by the English language.

The children try to help the scribe, and each other, by offering alternative versions of items. Tom's somewhat rambling explanation (51) is recast by Gavin in an attempt to help Nhishanth get something down. Nhishanth draws the session to a close and the final version was typed by him for public distribution (see Example four).

The final, published set of instructions

```
Instructions for the ambulance
crew.
   1. KNOWING WHERE TO GO.
   2. KEEPING BACK THE CROWDS.
    3. KEEP THEM BREATHING.
     4. STOP THEM BLEEDING.
       5. MAKE SURE THEYRE HEART IS
          BEATING.
        6. GIVE THEM BLANKETS.
         7. TAKE THEM TO THE
HOSPITAL.        8. DON'T TELL THEM
THEY ARE GOING
TO DIE.
     9. GIVE THEM A HOT WATER BAG.
      10. DON'T GIVE THEM TOO MUCH
DRINKS.
     11. CALL THE POLICE DIAL, 999.
      12. GO BACK TO THE AMBULANCE
STATION AND WARM UP.
```

Example 4

Conclusion

For these young children the act of authorship was so much more than just making a list. The authorship was a powerful act of meaning-making. The process of authorship was one where ideas were generated, exchanged, negotiated, refined, and finally put on paper. The balance between authoring activities involving the use of a writing implement and authoring activities involving thinking, was weighted heavily towards the thinking. This was not just because some of the children were fairly proficient when it came to putting text, in conventional ways, on to paper. Indeed, some of the children were not efficient in a conventional sense, as can be seen from Tom and Sally's draft instructions in Example 3. However, the limitations did not inhibit, in any way at all, the intellectual process of thinking about the development of a text. The children in these examples viewed the construction of a text as a thinking process. As a result of the transcripts I have been offered a special insight into the ways in which these children acted as authors.

It seems that if a group of young children is given the chance to take responsibility for their own learning and authorship then they will act in reasonable ways as authors. I have been surprised at the way the children have collaborated with each other and generally proved tolerant and supportive. This type of small group activity enables each child to play a significant role with individuals supplying ideas and motivation, even when aspects of their own literacy are not yet developed.

It also became apparent that the background discussion necessary for the creation of a text of rules can itself generate new knowledge and learning. The rationale used by the groups whilst engaged on their various activities and their perceived order of priority, reveals some sophisticated thinking. Frequently, it seems that children use the rule-making process to investigate their ideas of adult behaviour.

If the Dinosaur project first made me aware of the potential of 'rule-generation' for encouraging five- and six-year-old children to discuss and negotiate text, then the 'Dial 999' project reinforced and developed this insight. For those children, the act of devising and then publishing rules to govern behaviour was a valuable learning experience and through the use other children made of those rules, offered an important learning environment within the play area of our infant classroom.

—6— An author is a rat
Sue McCaldon and Linda Jones

Introduction

What are young children's understandings about authors? Four-year-old Danielle, when asked the question 'What is an author?' replied 'A rat'. Well, perhaps! But it is clear that in this case her understanding was very different from that of the teacher asking the question. It was this kind of response that influenced our decision to investigate further what young children understand about the authorship of books.

Background

As teachers of young children we work in two very different schools. One is situated in an inner city area and includes children from many different ethnic and social backgrounds. The children from this school are in a reception class and are either four- or five-years-old. The other school is located in a middle-class suburban area and has few ethnic minority children. These children are middle infants and are either five- or six-years-old.

One common link between our two classes is the emphasis given to being an author. Thus, the children are encouraged both to see themselves as authors and to take an interest in the authors of commercially produced books. There are a variety of ongoing activities in our classrooms which we hope increase the children's awareness of authorship. During shared reading times we talk about authors. We might say, for example, 'This book was written by Anthony Browne, didn't he write *Willy the Wimp*?' We also discuss whether the author and the illustrator are the same person. In both our classrooms there is an author's corner with materials freely available for children to make their own books. Some of these individual books, as well as stories produced during shared writing sessions, are 'published'. Classroom publication of books helps the children to see themselves as authors; the children can see their names in print just like a professional author. These books might also feature information about the authors such as their age and their interests.

The books we have published so far include stories based on real books, autobiographical details, children's own stories, recipe books, and instructions. High priority is also given to the authorship of messages and letters.

It was with these children, who had been immersed in this kind of literate environment, that we decided to investigate authorship. Now was the moment for truth!

Asking questions

We drew up a list of possible questions and decided that these would not necessarily be adhered to, depending on the children's responses. The questions were designed to establish what the children understood about authors, for example: What do authors do? Do you have to be a good speller to be an author? How old do you have to be? Is it easy? Can anybody be an author? Can a monkey or a computer be an author? We decided to talk to the children about authorship during everyday classroom situations, such as individual shared reading sessions. Thus, the normal classroom practice of mentioning the author of a book was extended by asking questions about authors generally. Rather than write down responses (which would have intruded on the session) we recorded each session and analysed the information later.

Naming authors

What emerged clearly from the questioning sessions was that most children, from both schools, were able to name at least one author. These were usually the authors of favourite books in the classroom. This would suggest that children, like ourselves, tend to remember the authors of books which they enjoy. One of the difficulties of questioning children is that however carefully the questions are phrased some children will find the situation threatening. This is particularly true of children whose first language is not English and their lack of response is not necessarily reflective of their knowledge and understanding. Situations in which the children initiate comments about authors can give greater insights into their understanding. This could be seen during a story-reading session with a group of four- and five-year-olds. The book, *The Enchanted Pig*, had been introduced and the author named as Tony Ross, when several children began to comment. Andrew said 'He wrote *I'm coming to get you* didn't he?' At this, Darren added 'He also wrote *The boy who cried wolf*'. Kelly contributed 'He's written lots of books' and Danielle asked pensively 'I wonder why he writes lots of books?'

From this exchange it can be seen that Andrew and Darren understand that an author can be someone who writes books. They also demonstrated their knowledge of other books written by the same author. Danielle's questioning of why Tony Ross writes lots of books may well be part of her attempts to make sense of the term author. Similarly Mamoon was trying to develop his understanding of 'author' when he asked 'Does the author make the books?' This is a particularly significant question for a young child. The relationship between objects and their origin is, from a young child's perspective, often rather obscure. Milk can appear to come from bottles not cows, seeds can appear to come from packets not flowers, and books can appear to originate from bookshops rather than authors. That there is a human creative hand behind books rather than some kind of divine creation, puts quite a different perspective upon the relationship a young child has with books and authorship.

Similar spontaneous incidents occurred with the five- and six-year-old children. During storytime when *Goodnight Owl* by Pat Hutchins was introduced, but before the author could be named, Douglas interrupted, saying 'It's by Pat Hutchins, she wrote *Titch* as well.' These examples show that the children are actively responding to the use of the term author and are reflecting on its meaning.

The children varied in their understanding of what authors actually do. Five-year-old Tariq, a bilingual child, commented on a book he was reading:

Tariq: It's by Tony Ross 'cos he's an author.
Teacher: If Tony Ross is an author what does he do?
Tariq: Brings books, he sleeps in a bed.

This conversation shows that Tariq can name an author and knows that there is a connection between authors and books. For Tariq, it would seem that the term author is somewhat abstract. Either he lacks a clear understanding of what an author does or is unable to explain it in English, his second language.

Importance of pictures

One recurring aspect in the children's comments was the author's involvement in the illustrations. Replies to questions revealed that an author is:

'someone who colours books'

'a person who can make books. A man that paints flowers and pictures'

'a person who writes books and draws pictures'.

These replies show the importance of pictures in books to young children and reflect the childrens' experiences with colourfully illustrated books. This is hardly surprising as many of the children are using the pictures to help them gain meaning from the text.

What authors do

Five-year-old Robert's understanding of what authors do is clearly linked to his own experience as the following dialogue shows:

Teacher: What is an author?
Robert: Anthony Browne.
Teacher: What does an author do?
Robert: Writes books, they make books.
Teacher: How do they make books?
Robert: By folding pieces of card and making pictures.

Other children demonstrated a more sophisticated view of the processes involved in authorship. The question 'Do authors have to be clever?' promoted discussion between a group of children. All the children thought authors were clever and some children's notion of cleverness appeared to be the ability to get things right first time:

Sarah: Because they have to be careful with the things that they do, they are not allowed to rub out.
Rebecca: 'Cos if they made a mistake and they rubbed it out it would come out all smudgy.

Katie: I think they can rub out.

Kirsteen: I think that first they would do the writing on a piece of paper, sort of like you did when we made 'Mark's messy room' and then you copied it out.

Kirsteen's comment is an indication of how she has used her own experiences to make sense of a situation beyond her knowledge; she shows a clear understanding of the revision process used in writing. Rebecca seems to think that authors write directly into books. This view was confirmed by other children. They were quite emphatic in reply to the question 'Do authors have to write neatly?' Heather said 'Yes, 'cos it's going to be in a book.' When asked how they thought the writing got into the book, Heather replied 'by computer'. Sarah said 'by felt tip pen'. These replies again reflect the children's own experiences as these are the methods used for classroom publication.

Heather has a clear idea of how to become an author:

'You have to write a book and send it off to a school or something.'

So authors please note, when you have finished folding your pieces of card, colouring the pictures and writing very neatly with your felt tip pens, please send your work to the nearest school for publication!

Can anybody be an author?

The children's views on whether a computer could be an author were somewhat mixed. Some thought that as a computer could write then it could be an author. Others indicated the importance of hands in the writing process. Anna said, 'No it can't write because it's got no hands or legs'. This attention to hands was reflected in one child's belief that monkeys couldn't be authors as they didn't have hands. As monkeys do have hands (well, paws) I queried this. The child's logical response was, 'Well my monkey doesn't have hands!'

None of the children thought that a monkey could be an author and gave various explanations. Two five-year-olds said:

Kelly: No, monkeys can't write . . . they haven't got the right sort of head.

Darren: No, they're pets, animals can't write.

and two six-year-olds said:

Anna: No...because monkeys are animals.

Heather: No, it can't write . . . it doesn't know where the pen is.

Heather's answer was investigated by asking if the monkey would be able to write if it was given a pen. Heather thought not but could not explain why. At this point Anna intervened:

Anna: It isn't a person.

Teacher: What is different between people and animals?

Anna: Because peoples got speech . . .

Sarah: . . . bubbles . . .

Anna: . . . people can talk and animals can't.

We were quite surprised at the sophistication of some of these answers. Sarah's interjection is again a reflection of classroom practices where speech bubbles are used in writing.

Children as authors

Generally the children had a positive view of themselves as authors. This could be seen both in questioning sessions and spontaneously in classroom situations. The idea for 'Andrew's Story' originated from the hospital play area in the classroom. Andrew's idea was developed by the class and written down by the teacher. The resulting 'published' big book, illustrated by the children, became part of the classroom library. During a storytime when the book was being read the children were asked 'Who is the author?' There was an immediate chorus of 'Class 7'. This response shows that the children see themselves as authors even when the teacher has done the writing. Another child's response illustrates this point. When talking about authors he said 'I'm an author, because I make lots of books. Mummy writes the words and I do the pictures. I tell her what to write.'

Although the children have a positive view of themselves as authors they also seem to distinguish between themselves and professional authors. Whilst five-year-old Darren is happy with the idea that he is an author he also thinks you have to be grown up:

Darren: I am an author.
Teacher: How old do you have to be to be an author?
Darren: You have to be a man.
Teacher: Can a lady be an author?
Darren: Oh yes.
Teacher: So you have to be grown up?
Darren: Yes.

A similar view was expressed by two six-year-old children who also felt that age was important:

Teacher: But you said you were an author.
Sarah: Five or six or seven or eight.
Heather: I don't think you would be one or two.

Is it easy to be an author?

When asked whether it would be easy to be an author all the children said 'Yes'. This view no doubt reflects the children's confidence in themselves as authors. However, there was a distinction between whether it was easy to be an author and whether authors found it easy to write. Most children felt that it was not easy for authors to write and their reasons for this differed:

Heather: No . . . you have to write it about that big *(indicating with her fingers a small size)*.
Kirsteen: No . . . you have to write neatly otherwise people wouldn't be able to read the book and if you spell words wrong the same would happen, you wouldn't be able to read the book.

These comments are concerned with the surface features of print. Other children felt that the difficulty was in getting ideas and with the content. Some children said authors got ideas from their head; they included themselves:

Anna: I made some stories up.
Teacher: Where did the idea come from?
Anna: Your head.

Andrew got his ideas from videos, but still recognised that there were difficulties: 'When I'm making a book, like a Moondreamer book, and I've got to do the clothes it's hard to remember what they look like.'

The question was phrased in such a way that it might be more readily interpreted to relate to professional authors. However, it was interesting to note that several children showed their belief in themselves as authors by relating the question to themselves.

Conclusion

Our initial aim in carrying out this investigation was to find out what children knew about book authors and book authoring. We recognised that a question and answer situation was not necessarily the best way to find out what children knew but, despite this drawback, we felt that our findings were supported by the spontaneous contributions which occurred in the classroom.

We found that the children had some understanding of what authors do; that they could name authors; use the term author naturally and had favourite authors; and that the author's role in illustrations is important. Our overriding impression was that the children had a positive view of themselves as authors. It was quite clear that the children based their views of authors upon their own experiences. We found little difference between the two classes except that the older children were better able to express themselves. In conclusion, we feel that by providing a classroom environment in which the children can be authors enables them to explore and build on their ideas of authorship.

Danielle may not have moved very far from her idea that an author is a rat, but she can be seen to be actively involved in trying to make sense of the term as her more recent plaintive query shows: 'Why do so many books have authors?'

—7— How much do children notice?
Janette Shearer

Janette Shearer

Introduction

Most schools have a notice-board. However, all too often they fulfil only a limited range of functions. Outside of schools, notice-boards tend to have different characteristics; characteristics which derive from the ways in which they constitute a meaningful and important feature in the lives of the people who use them.

One of their principal characteristics is that they just seem to grow and grow. As things occur, so items are added to the board and, as time passes, so the board tends to become overlaid with more and more items until someone decides – it has to be cleared. The whole process then starts all over again. Such a notice-board may be haphazard and it may be anything but neatly and formally laid out, but it is certainly dynamic. It reflects the way people actually live their lives and the concerns they genuinely have. In turn, people then use the notice-board to influence and control their own lives.

A typical notice-board at home may have coupons, stamps, notes, lists, letters, postcards, addresses, and many other items reflecting the day-to-day lives of people. Anyone in the family may add items to the board; it is owned by the whole family, not just a part of it.

The items on the board reflect the interests, attitudes, and values of a particular family. The coupons may reflect the economic status of the family; personal notes may reflect ebbs and flows in family relationships; letters and postcards will signify the network of family life. All these and many other aspects suggest that a notice-board is a highly functional and relevant way of using literacy.

Where the children of the family are concerned it is a wonderful demonstration of the 'why', 'when', 'where', and 'what' of literacy. They can see print arrive, see it selected, see it added to the board and can ask questions about it. They may contribute their own items either by creating items themselves or bringing home print or drawings from school. They are able to witness literacy being used in a dynamic, highly meaningful, and appropriate way.

Too many school notice-boards are the opposite of dynamic. They are often highly controlled; permission has to be granted before things can be placed upon them. They usually contain more formal items and those items are often placed on the board with the neatness and precision of a military display. The boards remain unchanged for long periods of time and the careful selection means that items are added relatively infrequently. They are often a repository for certain legalistic documents containing rules and regulations, and the usually faded and yellowed appearance of these suggests that the board is their permanent home. They all too seldom contain items written by children.

There are too many infant and nursery school notice-boards and classroom notice-boards which contain little else except a timetable or faded list of duties and monitors. Even the boards providing information for parents usually only contain the semi-legalistic matters of school uniforms, appeals and festivals. Once up they usually stay there.

It would seem that a wonderful opportunity is being missed for helping children, and maybe parents, extend their use, and their understanding, of literacy. Schools and classrooms should be full of dynamic notice-boards. What is going on in a school with no notice-boards – surely something is. Most schools are a bustle of fascinating activities and, although these may be represented through more conventional displays of work there is still something missing – the less formal dynamism of interaction mediated by literacy.

Our class notice-board

What I wanted to do was to offer the four- and five-year-olds in my class such an opportunity – to involve them in using print in so many stimulating and purposeful ways. The use of a notice-board in the classroom may even, I hoped, stimulate in the children and their families a sense of belonging to the school. I hoped it would help to foster genuine links between the school and the home – and perhaps even the community – while extending the children's understanding of literacy.

I set up the notice-board simply by providing materials (paper, card, pens, pencils, felt pens, and Blu-tack) and a prominent wall space backed with sugar-paper and labelled 'Our Notice-board'. I informed the children, and anyone else who wished to know, that this was our board and that they could use the materials and display on it anything they wanted to.

Notice-boards lend themselves to authorship of texts which lie outside the normally acceptable texts of school. They offer opportunities to generate messages, reminders, warnings, offers, claims, invitations, complaints and many other shorter types of text. How would the children in my class use it? Would it reveal an ability to handle these short texts in appropriate ways? I was interested to see what they felt was appropriate to display and at first I did not display anything on the board.

To begin with, the children used the board to display pictures and pieces of writing that they themselves had initiated in the classroom.

Example 1

Then some children started to bring in items they had created at home; some written with the help of members of their family or friends. The notice-board became covered with pictures, labelled drawings, diary entries, stories, home-made calendars and little booklets. Also commercially-produced items appeared; leaflets publicising various events that were to take place in the community – shows, theatre productions, films, displays to be held at the local library; posters advertising various products, such as double glazing; information sheets about local museums, parks, and leisure centres.

The children enjoyed displaying these items and were keen to show and share their contributions with other members of the class, parents, friends, and any other person who entered the classroom. The notice-board became a class talking-point. The various contributions were examined. Children asked each other questions about items that had been placed on the board. For a time commercially-produced leaflets fascinated the children. They wanted to know what they were about and whether they should be placed on the board. The leaflets stimulated talk about advertising, posters, signs, timetables, maps, places the children had visited and things they had seen and done.

One day, having forgotten to give out some letters at home-time the previous day, I asked the children what I could do to remind myself to give them out that afternoon. After various suggestions had been made we decided to write a reminder note and put it on the notice-board. This suggestion had been stimulated by one of the children who said that her mum made lists to help her remember things and that she put them on their home notice-board. Later this suggestion provoked a discussion about notice-boards at home.

This discussion was interesting in that it revealed to me that the children had varying concepts of what a notice-board was, who owned them, and what purpose they served. Could a notice-board be pictures and cards stuck on a wall? What about notes stuck on a fridge door; pictures, letters and cards pinned on a board on a bedroom wall; notes stuck on a window or wall next to the telephone; notes clipped together and hung beneath a cupboard; or writing on calendars? What were these notes about and what purposes did they serve? One boy had a definite idea of what his family notice-board was used for. He described it as hanging on the kitchen wall, with cards on it from the dentist and doctor, postcards from relations, a leaflet about Sale Water Park which told his dad how to get there, and drawings of his that his mum had pinned up. We considered whether we had any similar items on our notice-board.

From then on notes from parents excusing children from school for particular appointments were placed on the board, and some children wrote their own reminder notes indicating when they had doctor or dentist appointments.

As we were involved in a class theme on 'Time' I also decided to place a weekly appointments list on the notice-board, with a section for appointment notes for each day of the week. Our class TV programme times, PE and hall times were written down on cards and placed under the appropriate days. Times when visitors were expected and dates of visits out of school were also noted and displayed.

Children began to write their own reminder notes or to ask me for help with them.

Please remember to put the rubbhg

Example 2

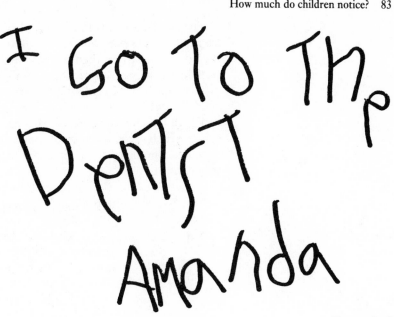

I GO TO THe DenTST

Amanda

Example 3

One child who clearly didn't want to forget the change from his dinner money was very insistent that I help him to write a note reminding me to give him his change.

Remember to give

me   my   dinner money

Louis

Example 4

It became a ritual to survey the notice-board at home-time just in case we had anything to remember. Postcards, photographs, and posters also started to appear on the board and each morning adults and children alike became interested in items placed on it. The addition of the weekly school menu interested many parents; and I also placed each day's TV programme pages from *Radio Times* and *TV Times* on the board, which prompted a keen response from the children to ask what was on the television that day.

The children also started a postal system. It all began when one child suggested that a party invitation for an absent child could be stuck onto the notice-board and then the absent child would see it when she came back to school. Subsequently, the children regularly posted invitations, birthday and seasonal cards on the board.

They began to make cards and write letters and messages to each other and stick these on the notice-board next to invitations and other commercially-produced cards. Inevitably, most of these notes and cards were taken home by the recipient. Most of the ones I possess are those sent to me.

To mrsI Love you sometime my mum let me in her bed I enjoyed writeing this letter

Love Foom emma
xxxx

Example 5

To Mrs shearer everybody loveyou from mumd Ad DaVid Ashley Anty cyinno Andrew I love you

Example 6

OT

kirstey

I HPY MY HPBA HMohh A nok ko mo
love
AMd hdo

Example 7

The children greatly enjoyed posting messages to each other on the board and waiting for them to be claimed. If the writer became impatient, hints were dropped to the intended recipient of the message. Children made their own envelopes, and curious looking packages appeared on the notice-board, addressed to particular members of the class. I myself wrote messages to the class about events or activities which were going to occur during the day or following day. Messages which arrived from other teachers in the school, together with letters from parents and other adults, were also placed on the notice-board, as were lists of things the children could bring from home relating to class or school activities.

It wasn't long before I noticed that the children always posted these items in one area of the notice-board. There seemed to be an unspoken rule that particular items would be placed in particular spaces on the board – one area for appointments and reminders; another for messages, cards, invitations and letters; and an area where the dinner menu and TV programme times were posted. They seemed to be organising the space on the board for particular purposes.

Throughout the day the children used the board: referring to it for information such as what was for dinner, posting and claiming messages, displaying personal items and other items that interested them, and pinning up sign-up sheets and questionnaires requiring other people to respond to them.

rIt yor naM
to the snake

uugoou Helpy
kirstey coRnE

Example 8

These four- and five-year-old children were using the print-related items on the notice-board in appropriate ways and were well aware of the audience they were reaching and the purpose of the items placed on the board in this social context.

The children's awareness of their audience was vividly demonstrated when a group of children decided to start their own notice-board on the outside of our classroom door. When I asked them why they had started a board there, one child informed me that the other classes and other grown-ups would then be able to read their messages.

The children used the notice-board for their own ends, and often incorporated its use into role-play situations – as when several children set up a travel agency using the notice-board to display the advertised cards for the holidays (one child informed me that one of the cards said 'Go to Spain for 80p!').

Throughout this period, the children continued to display personal articles created by themselves. One child posted a story bit by bit as she wrote it over a period of several days. The class waited for the next episode as each part was written on a card and posted in sequence on the notice-board.

Naturally, the board was used at some times more than others. On one occasion, in particular, the board had become so cluttered that the children had begun to stick notices on top of other notices. Then, when a squabble arose between two children, one of whom had covered the other child's notice with her own, I felt it was time to have a class talk about how this problem could be solved. The children were already removing outdated menus and TV programme sheets from the board because they had served their purpose, so it was decided to extend this practice to other items, so that notes relating to events that had occurred would be removed. It was also agreed that if there was still not enough space, personal items such as pictures and stories which had been displayed for over a week would be removed too. In this way, the children were further encouraged to manage the notice-board for themselves.

Conclusion

The extent to which the children were organising and ordering information on the notice-board pleasantly surprised me – it showed how even children as young as four or five could use print for a wide range of purposes to suit their own requirements. I was pleased to observe how setting up the notice-board had provided a situation in which the children could display their literacy knowledge and skills in appropriate and practical contexts. Also, the notice-board helped to foster home/school links – parents and other adults became more involved in the children's daily school activities. Thus it could be said that the notice-board helped initiate parental involvement.

By contributing to the notice-board the children were able to legitimately generate an extremely wide range of short texts that had clear significance within the context of the classroom and school. With those texts the children had been able to control and influence behaviour; they had been able to make, and break, friendships; they had ensured that others were kept informed of classroom news and events; they had offered salutations and greetings; they were able to chide, scold, and reprimand; and they were able to extend invitations and reply to requests. By using the notice-board frequently and in appropriate ways many effective, yet often ignored, aspects of authorship were attempted by the children. The setting up of the notice-board in the classroom had enabled the children to demonstrate and extend their abilities as authors in their own right.

—8— But we still believe in Father Christmas
Anne Robinson

Anne Robinson

Introduction

When I started teaching a class of thirty second year infants in September 1986 I was determined to put into practice many of the ideas I had discussed with student teachers over the previous twelve years in college. Major changes had taken place in thinking about the development of literacy, and in my own beliefs, since I last had a class of my own. I could not return to copy-writing or the use of repetitive reading schemes. The children were encouraged to take more responsibility for the choice of books to read and topics to write about. Copy-writing was not allowed and at all times children had to use their own resources to spell words. Invented spelling was encouraged. They could spend as much time as they wanted on a piece of writing; they could return to it or discard it as they wished.

The 'witch' stories

Among other things, I tried to encourage story writing through both suggestions and more structured activities. For example, at Halloween we had discussed the idea of writing 'witch stories'. Some time was spent thinking and collecting ideas, about what witches looked like, where they might live and what they might do. The results were, on the whole, encouraging in so far as they included descriptions of what witches looked like, where they lived and what they did! In other words, the children were responding to the situation as they saw it, but it was one which had been carefully directed by me. The three examples which follow illustrate the range of writing ability found within the class.

Robert had shown in discussion that he was aware of appropriate content and that he had relevant experience of such stories. His ability to translate these into a written story was limited by his skill in capturing words in print:

Robert (5 yrs 2 mths)

Translation:-

I. h. s. e. w.

I have seen a witch

His response was a statement recorded in initial letters. Yet we must not underestimate the effort which went into the production of those five letters. Robert wrote what *he* wanted to say rather than limiting himself to 'safe' copied words.

More confident authors set their descriptions in continuous prose. Many children reflected their experience of story in their choice of openings: 'Once upon a time'; 'In a dark, dark, wood'; 'A long time ago'. Some children made a good start, but provided no satisfactory conclusion, while others indicated their understanding of composition by producing brief but well-rounded stories. Tom and Sally, for example, illustrate the ability to organise the elements into a coherent whole.

Tom (5 yrs 9 mths)

wgib magi

Sii lviv in a LiLte
cotgi.
Sii look lac a wbo weitt
wn doe wgib mgii soi
a boy and she flew
over teh boy
she jusb kacub
and she lanbib she had a nice
bay

Translation:

Wicked Maggie

She lived in a little
cottage.
She looked like a wicked witch
one day wicked maggie saw
a boy and she flew
over the boy
She just cackled
and she landed she had a nice day.

Sally (5 yrs 7 mths)

A long time ago there lived a
witch and her name was
cackle. and she had a black
cat. and she had a black
hat. and she lived in A
cottage. one day she made
a spell it was wrong
She gave it to the Red witch. the
Red witch drank it. the Red witch
died.

On reflection I realised that the pre-writing discussion had imposed a particular view of what counted as a story, and what counted as the contents of a story; this led most of the children to interpret the story-writing task in a similar way. They knew I would accept their own attempts at spelling and for the most part they used their phonic knowledge to represent words which they could not recall visually. This should have freed them to write what they wanted to say. However, in most cases they restricted themselves to writing about those things which had been discussed. The content was bound, or at least greatly constrained, by what they thought I wanted; after all, we had discussed at length the kinds of things suitable for inclusion. Unknown to them I wanted more, and I certainly anticipated that the children would be able to build on these early efforts to attempt more adventurous story creations. This did not happen.

I had imagined that the children's rich experience of literature would reflect more obviously in their writing. It *was* obvious in their conversation about books; it *was* obvious in the way they used their knowledge of literary language to anticipate and predict in their reading and in the way they re-enacted story events in their play. Yet they did not *choose* to author stories.

The problem of 're-tellings'

One day a child started to re-tell the story of *The Three Little Pigs*. This was the first major breakthrough in writing at length. The event was notable for the intense concentration and the willingness of the child to continue with the story over a three-day period. It was also notable for the enthusiastic reaction on my part. Other children were obviously impressed by the amount of writing produced and many followed the lead. But they all re-told *The Three Little Pigs* as well! Of course, I was pleased, but it took all my acting ability to react with the same degree of enthusiasm to the fifteenth re-telling of the same story.

Paul's 'Three Pigs' story is typical of the children's writing during the re-telling phase. It is not reproduced in full, as readers will be more than familiar with the plot.

Paul (5 yrs 6 mths)

Once a pon atime one Little
pig ascd The mumm pig if He
Cod gow and The wolf wont
get me and he met a Man
caring sume sudraw He sed
can I have sume sudrow
Yes sed The man you hove it
and thankyoy and he begean
to bee gan to bild his
house it wos nays but it
waso not veriy srog and The
wolf ceme a log anb he Little
pig Little pig Let me ceme in No No
not bay may chiny chin
chin wit not Let you cume in
The wolf sed well I ll Huff and
Puff and blow yr howse bone

In this extract the story form and sequence can be seen. It is faithful to the traditional tale in that it tells the story partly through direct speech. The well known 'I'll huff and I'll puff and I'll blow your house down', and 'No, no, by the hair of my chinny, chin, chin' form major repetitive elements throughout the story.

This approach to authoring stories has both advantages and disadvantages for young writers. Re-telling reduces the burden of composition; as long as the child can remember the story all he has to do is write it down. He does not have the added problem of thinking what to say since that is already prescribed for him. *The Three Little Pigs* and other traditional tales often have a repetitive element, which means that having transcribed one part the writer can actually copy out that part again later in the story. This can be wonderfully relaxing in a classroom where copying is not allowed! In addition, the sense of pride in producing so much text should not be underestimated. However, a disadvantage of re-telling is that once committed to a particular story there is no escape. The story is set for you and cannot be changed, at least not before the skill of summarising has developed. There is no way that 'and they went home to bed' can be used to draw to a close a story which is taking too long to write. 'I can't think what to put next' can not be used as an excuse for avoiding writing any more. I was to witness many a look of resigned frustration as children realised that they had produced a whole page of writing and had still only reached 'the house of straw'! These children had no problem with thinking like the book; their problem was that they felt the story had to be told exactly like the book.

'Re-telling' and 'reality'

It had occurred to me that I could use the children's achievements in re-telling stories by encouraging the idea of writing 'the further adventures' of various well known characters. But of all the things I tried to stimulate in class this was the most resounding failure. Conversations went something like this:

Teacher: I know you like Goldilocks and the Three Bears, perhaps you could write another story about her.
Child: *(No response.)*
Teacher: What do you think she did after she had been to the three bears' house?
Child: I don't know

or

Teacher: Shall we write a new story about Little Red Riding Hood?
Child: I don't know any.

I was frustrated to say the least. I had a group of children who ought to have been authoring their own stories; they had the confidence to write at length and the ability to sustain concentration over a long period. They also had wide experience of a variety of stories. What was the problem? Did I have a group of able but totally unimaginative children? Clearly, this was not the case as the children displayed imagination and creativity in all other areas of the curriculum. Observation of their behaviour while playing with a wide variety of materials and toys, and particularly in the 'structured play' area of the classroom, showed that they were able to 'create story' to act as a framework for imaginative play. The root of the problem had to be elsewhere.

Had I thought more carefully about my children and been less concerned with developing a particular style of writing, the answer might have been revealed more easily. I should have remembered their excitement leading up to Christmas and the looks on their faces when

Father Christmas appeared in person at their party in December. I should have recognised the clues in their reaction to another activity taking place as a result of using *The Jolly Postman* book. Each child had chosen a fairy story character to write to and had received a reply written in character. On the day the replies arrived the children were highly excited and many rushed to respond immediately. From their reactions and comments it was obvious that most of them believed the letters and cards had actually been written by the characters. Their behaviour reinforced suggestions that young children think story characters are real; that stories are reports of real events which, even though they have happened 'over the hills and far away' or 'a long, long, time ago' are, nevertheless true.

Only one child came to me and asked 'Who really wrote the letter, it wasn't Sleeping Beauty, was it?' 'Who do you think it was?' I asked. 'I think it was you,' she said with a smile. Although this conversation raised doubts in some children's minds the majority held firmly to the belief that they had been in touch with Fairyland; their belief having been supported quite recently by presents appearing in stockings on Christmas Eve. It is a brave five-year-old who challenges the very thing which brings such rewards.

In retrospect it is possible to interpret the responses of the children who 'did not know what to do' when asked to create a new story for an existing character. Perhaps what they really meant was that they did not 'know' any other stories about those characters; that no one had yet told them what happened to Goldilocks when she went home from the woods. To ask a child who really believes in story characters to create a story about them is to make the world very problematic. Even when children understand that books have authors, it is possible that some children think of those authors as merely reporting rather than creating. Of course authors do report – they draw on memories, they observe behaviour and they transcribe stories from the oral tradition – but they also create stories based on characters who could be real, doing things which could happen, in places which could exist. Others create stories involving characters, events and environments which are pure fantasy.

My children were certainly authors in the sense that they had moved away from copying and had engaged in reflection upon what they wrote and how they wrote. They had engaged in the decision-making process during reporting on their experiences and also while re-telling known stories. However, it seems as if these children still had to realise that stories grew initially inside authors' minds, in the same way that ideas for play grew inside their own minds. The realisation did come, for some children, by the end of the school year. Whether this was a result of maturing awareness or as a result of varied experiences in class, it is impossible to say.

The 'one-eyed monkey' stories

Later in the year (as part of a book week) I drew the children's attention to an old dusty wooden box which contained a random collection of objects. On the lid of the box was a notice which said 'All the things in this box are sad because they have no story to belong to. Can you make them happy?' Of course, it was a variation on an old theme as a stimulus for writing. The objects included, among other things, a clown's red nose, a bag of gold coins, and a bunch of keys. Also, there was a monkey puppet with only one eye. This trivial little toy proved to be the key which I had been searching for all along. Without any direct instruction, with no compulsion to write monkey stories, and with no pre-writing discussion the children identified with the monkey and, in their writing, gave him a life of his own. Most of the monkey stories were quite different from those attempted previously.

The first examples show little advance on the 'witch stories' although, for the individuals concerned, represent significant development. Robert's story compares most favourably with his previous attempt. He gives his story a title, provides an explanation for the lost eye, describes what the monkey did as a result of his accident and resolves the tale happily. His increased ability to capture words in print and his use of phonic spelling allows him to write his simple chaining of events with confidence.

Robert (5 yrs 9 mths)

the myciy wif one ay

the myciy Fel down of the
mawhtin wen the myciy
Fel to the dotRE ten He got
up to luc Fu His Iy wen
Hi Fdwnd his Iy Hiy went
dac Howm His myn and
dad glrewd his Iy on

Translation:

the monkey with one eye

the monkey fell down off the
mountain when the monkey
fell (he went) to the doctor then he got
up to look for his eye when
he found his eye he went
back home His mum and
dad glued his eye on

Paul's story, although brief, has the makings of a mini tragedy. After the traditional opening he uses the word 'brilliant' and the repetitious reference to climbing to give a picture of an able-bodied, happy monkey. His choice of 'thorn bush' for the cause of the accident is most suitable in this context. The sad ending contrasts sharply with the introduction and is somewhat unusual, as most of the children resolved their story happily.

Paul (5 yrs 10 mths)

Once upon A time there wos
A mccee and he wos briyont
at claymeeg trees
and claymeeg fenses
he lacd clameeg theigs
one dey he clamd up a ton
both and a thon suc in his eye
he fell done and his eye
come ote and he wos cold
the muceey with one eye
and he codn clam a tree agen

Tom, although beginning his story imaginatively, aptly describes the reality of the situation by placing the monkey and the chest in the classroom context. This provides an interesting mix of fantasy and reality organised into story form. The introduction of 'chapter', although not really appropriate, is a clear reflection of his own reading of longer texts as is the use of 'the end'. It is also an illustration of his view of himself as an author; someone who can write stories like stories in books.

Tom (5 yrs 11 mths)

One upon a Time there was a litteL
monKey one day he was walking along and his
eye was lose and it fell out (chapter two)
and he fell Down and he found himself
in a chest the next day someone found
the chest and took it. then she cept it
and put the chest on a table and she kept
putting thinings in the chest soon she
got fed up with the chest soon she sent
It away to a school the school called
the chest the story chest and the
monkey lived Happliy ever after the End

Helen's story could, with very little editing, take its place alongside any number of stories written for young children. It clearly reflects her own experience of reading the kind of repetitive fairy-tale where a host of characters join in a search, asking the same question over and over again. The story is told partly through description and partly through direct speech. She explains that the monkey was sad, the inference being that this was because he had lost an eye, and returns to this theme after giving the monkey a place to live and a large family. This family is necessary for the wide scale search for the eye. Brothers, sisters and cousins search high and low, and ask all kinds of characters for help before the eye is found and all ends happily. The only unresolved issue is Billy's motive for sending them to 'people in the street' when he had the eye all the time.

Helen (6 yrs 7 mths)

Once upon A Time Ther
was A monkey with
one eye it was
very sad it was
called one eyed sandy
because iT had one
eye IT lived on A
hill with its
        BROTHERS and
SISTERS
and iT had 12
Cousins six boys
and six giRls one
day one eyed
Sandy ThougHt
I can HaRdly
do enithing
with only one
eye so he went

to his 12 cousins
and said Please will
you Help me
Find my eye and
His 12 cousins
SAid yes
So THey split up
Six went on the
sbRancH and six
looked on THe
gRound but they
cud noT Find it
BuT tHey would noT
give up so The
one eyed Sandy
SAid leTs go and
Tell my BROTHERS
and SISTERS
one eyed SAndy
SAid to iTS
broTHERS and
sisTers Please
will you Help me
find my eye
So one eyed SAndys
BROTHERS and
SISTERS SAid
Yes we SHAll
Help you find
your eye one of ITS
Cousins called Billy
SAid wy dont we
go and ask some
poeple in the STREET
So They all went
to THe BuHcers
and SAid Have you
seen my eye know
I HAVE noT seen
YouR eye But you
can go and ask THe
DOCTERS if THey
HAVe seen youR
eye so They all went
to THE DOCTERS and
one eyed SAndy sAid
Have you seen my
eye I THink Billy
THe monkey HAs
goT your eye
BUT weRe is He
he is on THAT
TREE so THey
CLimbed THe TRee
and got tHe
eye back.

Edwina reveals in her story how she wrote herself into a problem and then thought of a way round it. Her story is essentially being created as it is written, so after the visit to the doctors and the arrival at the pond she has an idea that this is an appropriate place for the eye to be found. However, in order for it to be found, it had to get there in the first place. There is no reason at all for Edwina to write in the reason if she is writing solely for herself; she already knows. The reason she has put in the explanation 'Once before he went for a walk the same way' is because she is conscious of there being other readers who may not be privy to this information. Thus, her belated reference to the possible cause of the loss of the eye is an example of an author's sensitivity to the needs of her readers. A similar instance occurs later in the story when a friend is written in. Edwina's responses are crude and she has yet to appreciate the potential of redrafting something that is uncomfortable but, nevertheless, it reveals an awareness of the duty of an author to make some concessions to the people who will read their texts.

Edwina (5 yrs 11 mths)

Once upon a time there
was a monkey and
it only Had one eye
and one day he went
for a walk he went
to the docter to
see if he had
seen it and he said
no sorry so he went
out of the docters and
went out on his walk and
he found a pond. and
once before he went for a walk
the same way and the eye
dropd in the pond
and he did not no how to get
the eye out he could not
dive in can I he said
to him slef then he found
behide him a friend of his
and they went back to
his house and they sat
down to think how to
get his eye out. they
went for a walk and
they new they had forgot
somethink they went back
home to get the fishing net

the end

The two final examples show children writing at greater length and orchestrating the elements of story with great imagination.

Hannah demonstrates many interesting strategies in her story telling. After the traditional opening, her monkey is introduced, named, housed and described as lonely. Loneliness is a recurrent theme throughout the story; it provides the reason for escape from the toy box (a new name for the 'chest'), the need to obtain another monkey and the feelings of the second monkey alone in the pet shop. The story is told partly through description and partly through direct speech, for example, 'I am going to escape', 'I forgot my teddy bear' (although conventional speech marks are not used). The teddy bear plays a minor role but was not forgotten as he appeared in the pictures which showed the monkey at school. Hannah has a story-teller's feel for language, which she demonstrates when she writes 'luckily the lid was open'; 'he was lonely. So lonely that ...'; and in the final section 'and from that day to this the monkeys have never been seen'. She also has the ability to capture quite accurately the language of my classroom as she recalls the routines of asking questions of the children and organising group work. She has successfully woven real life material into the context of imaginative story telling.

Hannah (6 yrs 1 mth)

Once upon a Time Ther was a
mokey a mokey with oneeye. the monkey
was called Sandy. He lived in a toy box.
it was very lonlee one athtenoon
it thort I am going to escap.
luckilaye the lid was open he hered
awt and went to the boor and went.
in the hall.

I fogot my tedy bear seab
Sandy. He hered to the box and got the
ted y bear and ran awt sid and went
up a tree and swang from sid to sid
ho sead the children a monkey they
trid to cach him.

and wille he swang he did not
see the children triing to get
him. up the three they hab labas and
they was climing up them . and
the ciledren got himand carid
him to school and the teecher
let vicky show him to the class
and they made him ther pet.and put him
in a caje

he was very lonly. so lonly that
the techer sead I will get a nuver
monkey and I will make namese for
them and Helen Sally and Vicky
and Racheal to p.ut ther hanes
up and Mrs Robinson sead Sally
Sandy saed Sally. and Mrs
Robinson sead I will Rite
it dowen and I wil get a nuver
monkey from the pet shop.

and that nigh Mrs Rodin son went
to the petshop and bort a monkey
it was just like Sandy and it was in a
caje and it was loking very sad it was
thinking wate a shcool wud be like.

Mrs Robinson took the monkey home
and put the caje dowen ho she cride the teacher

went back to the pet shop and
bort some monkey food and went home
made the tea and went to woch tely
dad came home as soon as the telly
had finished. and they had tea and
went to bed. nex bay Mrs Robinson got
up and went to school with the monkey
she went up Mishill at last she came
to the school. She took of her kote, and
then she saed red groop go in the play room
Blue groop go to the craft tabel Green groop
go to the Mathes tabel Yellow groop go to the
raking tabel orinj groop go to Mis Miny

Wen the teacher went. the tow monkeys
saw that the door was opon Sandy saed
shal we escape yes saed the uver monkey
so they went owte of the caje and went to
the door and went owt in to the playgrownd
they went up a tree and swang from branch
to branch and wen they got to the gate they
went down the tree and jumued over the
thens and went up Mis hill and went to
the pet shop the pet man saw them and
from that day to this the monkies have
nether been sonede

Sally's story offers a traditional opening, but not such a traditional
ending! Sally reflects her knowledge of story in what starts as a typical
adventure story with sexual stereotyping. The change comes on the last
page where Sandy becomes the active and most decisive character.

Sally (6 yrs 2 mths)

Once there was a monkey
and she was called Sandy.
She had a boy-frend he
was called Andy. One day
they were going to the zoo.
Sandy packed the food
and Andy got the car
ready. they got in the car
and drove away. the
monkeys krept in to
the zoo fist Sandy got
a Guide around the zoo
then Andy got 2 ice creams
first they went to see
their monkey cousins
as soon as the 2 monkeys
saw three cousins they
Jumped up for Joy. Sandy
and Andy got into the cage
and they had some food

whit their cousins. Aftra
they had been to see cousins
they went to see the crocadil
when they to the crocadil house
Sandy and Andy climbed up
the wall.
When they climded up the
wall Sandy and Andy looked down
and Andy fell in. the crocadil went
Snap Snap Snap Andy felt
his eye ik wasn't there he called
for Sandy qwiqley Sandy got
a rope out of her pokit
Shde throw ik down for Andy
Andy climded up.
We must get out of
here said Sandy as she Dragged
Andy out she put him in
the car and drove away.
When theyt got home Andy
said what shall I do
I have only got one
eye we can't by one
and I can't make
one. and I can't have
a boy-frend with only
one eye so Sandy Left and
she fon od a monkey that
was called pandy and they
got marrid and they
lived happley ever after
and Andy was throwed out.

Sally introduces her characters and sets the scene, a trip to the zoo. This is expanded by giving details of the preparation for the day out. The circumstances of their entry to the zoo are implied in her choice of the word 'crept'. She uses a series of common-place activities to effectively build up to the climax of the accident (most appropriately situated in the crocodile pit). From this point on Sally gives the reader a much clearer view of the characters of the two monkeys. This is not developed through direct description but through the characters' actions and speech. The ending is curious. Most children's stories end happily. Here we have, in effect, a tragedy. Andy is discarded for a 'complete' monkey. We have been prepared for this by the apparently heartless comment 'I can't have a boyfriend with only one eye' but there is an interesting touch in the way Sally follows the line 'they lived happily ever after' by the stark 'and Andy was thrown out'.

Conclusion

Following the 'monkey stories' the children went on to write many more of increasingly varied kinds. In fact, it was difficult to get them to write anything other than stories for some time. They still had a lot to learn about being authors. It can be seen from the examples of the children's work that spelling and punctuation are still developing. The children need more experience of organising the texts, and need engagement in discussions about redrafting and editing. However, the children had made a major discovery, a discovery of funadmental importance to all those who would aspire to write fiction; stories are not predetermined, they are created inside authors' minds. When they recognised this – the children recognised themselves as authors. I cannot claim to have taught the children this and find it impossible to say why they made the move to become authors of this kind just when they did. It could have been the culmination of literary experiences provided at home and school; or it could have been the developing confidence in themselves as writers. Alternatively, it could have been that they were almost ready to stop believing in Father Christmas; the dawning realisation that fantasy is not real and that it can be created and controlled in texts by people and, more particularly, people like themselves.

—9— Shared writing

Georgina Herring

Introduction

My experience as a teacher of primary aged children has led me to believe that children learn best when they are allowed to investigate materials in their environment, and when they are allowed to experiment freely. However, I also believe that this exploration can be combined with access to positive demonstrations of learning. I have found, on a number of occasions, that involving parents on equal terms in their children's education has been extremely effective in promoting interest and learning. Thus, it seems to me that parents are in an ideal position to interact with children's exploration and investigation of the world. Their experience with their own children usually means that they are able to operate with children in the classroom in extremely sensitive ways.

Teachers are now well used to involving parents in the literacy education of their children, and the school in which I was teaching as a middle infant teacher was already committed to shared reading involving the use of 'real' books. The teachers had also begun to develop book-making within the classrooms, and all book corners included a wealth of books written, illustrated, and produced by the children themselves. The school, as part of its policy, was making substantial and successful efforts to increase parental participation and offered good access to parents, held plentiful meetings and social occasions, and had begun to hold literacy-related sessions, not simply to explain school policy but to involve the parents in the formal education of their children.

It was during the school's development into partnership with parents, that I was able to view a video, made in Dorset by the National Writing Project, which seemed to pick up many of the issues that were important to both myself and the school. The teacher featured in this video, Simon Adorian, had arranged for his class of ten-year-old children to write with parents, and produce books for three- and four-year-old children. Having seen his ten-year-olds perform very successfully, I wondered whether I would be able to carry out a similar project with my much younger children. Most of the children I taught were aged five, although a small number had recently passed their sixth birthday. I felt that if I was able to involve a group of parents in making books with my children, then they would benefit from the uninterrupted one-to-one assistance from an adult who would listen to them, scribe for them and, through the interaction, provide demonstrations of how such books could be authored. I also felt that the parents might benefit from such close involvement with the children in a task which would probably make considerable demands upon all the participants.

I realised that it would be difficult to simply use the parents of the children in my class; many of them would be at work during the day. I therefore circulated a letter to all parents of children in the school requesting help with a writing project which would operate one afternoon a week for about six weeks. Parents were also invited to bring along their own pre-school children to be the audiences for the book we were going to write. It was important that my children would be able to meet with, and talk to, the children for whom they were going to be writing.

It was also important that I had clear time to explain the project to the parents who had responded, and fortunately colleagues agreed to take my class between them for some story sessions after playtimes. This allowed me to hold two one-hour sessions with the twenty-one parents who turned up. We watched extracts from the Dorset video. I explained what the parents' role was to be: making a book with a child from my class for their own younger child or a child in the school's nursery class. We looked at class-made books and talked about how the children would be the authors and illustrators and the adults simply the facilitators. We had a go at some writing ourselves and tried our hands at making books. Some parents expressed fears about their own handwriting and spelling. Others questioned the amount of direction they would be expected to give to the children. This meeting was really useful in helping parents understand the commitment required and to air any doubts.

The first meeting with the children and the parents was a complex affair. We had to spread into two rooms and I managed to get local help to run a small crèche for the younger children brought along by the parents. During this session my children were introduced to their 'readers' and invited to talk to them about the kind of stories they liked. Each parent worked with one child (in some cases two) and during the following four sessions, all the attention and effort went into the generation of text, illustrations and the production of the book.

Writing together

The success of this project hung on the nature of the relationship between the parents and the children. It would clearly be of limited help to the children if the parents acted purely as scribes, making no suggestions, offering no thoughts and never inviting the children to reflect upon what they had written. My hope was that the ways in which the parents worked with the children would help the children understand that authorship carried with it certain kinds of responsibilities both towards the text and the reader.

Because this project was carried out as part of our school's involvement in the National Writing Project, we were able to use their facilities to video as much of, and as many of, the sessions as possible. The videos were general in nature but they allowed access to some of the interactions which occurred. Although few in number, they give some insight into how the children and parents worked together. In the following transcripts P is always the parent.

P: *(Reading)* 'When I got out of the car my brother and sister were asleep so I had to shake them. Then the car went on its own. It peeped its horn at people.' Now what shall we say?

G: And . . . and when it got home . . .

P: Hmm.

G: Er . . . it . . . it . . . it can . . . it can . . . the man can get out.

P: The man can get out?

G: And . . . and right, it's an invisible man.

P: Oh in the car. Is it Mr Nobody in the car?

G: No and . . . and . . . right . . . the man is invisible and he goes and gets out of the car.

P: Hmm.

G: Opens . . . goes . . . climbs . . . walks through the door.

P: Hmm.

G: He goes . . . he walks through the other door. The man goes upstairs he wakes Mum and Dad up...he takes them to work and goes . . . and then they come back and they work in the pub . . . go upstairs . . . get . . . get . . . get in the . . . go and tell the invisible man go and get me us and he gets us and he go and gets us . . . comes back . . . tells us . . . goes . . . comes...he goes in and we go in right.

P: Hmm.

G: And then we watch telly and go to bed and in the morning we watch telly again.

P: But who's this man though?

G: The invisible man.

P: Oh I see. So we've got an invisible man in the car as well . . . does he sit in the driving seat?

G: No . . . yeah . . . yeah he sat in the driving seat.

P: So . . . he's driving the car then . . . it's not driving on its own?

G: It . . . it is driving on its . . . but . . . we think it's driving it on its own but we don't know it's an invisible man.

P: Oh I see so there's an invisible man.
      (Writes) 'There . . . is . . .'

G: And we . . . a man drove us to school and 'cos we thought it was driving on its own.

P: *(Continues writing)* 'a man . . . driving . . . the . . . car . . .' And can you see the invisible man?

G: No we don't know its an invisible man.

P: I see.
      (Writes) 'and . . . no . . . one . . . can . . . see . . . him . . .'

G: *(At dictating speed)* Only its mate.

P: Oh! Has it got a mate as well?

G: *(Nods)*

P: Right . . . *(writing)* 'only its mate . . . only . . . its . . . friend'

G: Can . . . see . . . him . . .

P: And is the car its friend?

G: Yeah . . . we don't know that it's his friend . . . they just . . . we

don't know that it's his friend.
P: Right . . . OK.

In this extract the parent demonstrates the sensitivity with which the parents approached their involvement with the children. She keeps the child on track by re-reading what has been composed, she gently encourages the child to go on composing, and quietly asks questions which allow the child to clarify what is being composed. In the way she asks questions, she helps remind the child that there is a demand to make things explicit for readers. Her questions 'Is it Mr Nobody in the car?'; 'But, who's this man though?'; 'So he's driving the car then . . . it's not driving on its own?' invite the child to reconsider the clarity of his text. There is no sense of instruction and there is no sense of a view being forced upon a child, something which is prevalent in many classrooms.

Similar sensitivity is found in this next extract which also reveals very clearly the extent to which the child is drawing on his own book reading experiences. The child is, in effect, engaging in a re-telling, rather than the construction of an original story.

D: *(Referring to a book)* Stegosaurus eats all the plants.
P: How do you spell it?
D: S . . .
P: *(Refers to book for word)* Ate . . . all . . . the . . . plants.
D: Yeh . . . he ate 98 cabbages, 99 cabbages, and 100 cabbages;
     (P writes as Dale tells her) 98 cabbages.
P: And after 98 cabbages?
D: Ninety-nine cabbages and then 100 cabbages.
P: What happened then?
D: Tyrannosaurus rex came out of her egg.
P: We've already said that haven't we here? Just a minute . . . *(refers to text)*.
D: Yeh.
P: So we can't really say that.
D: Tyrannosaurus wanted to eat them all.
P: *(Writing)* 'wanted . . . to . . . eat . . . them . . . all'. Shall we make that a reason for something?
D: Mmm?
P: Mmm . . . a reason why?
D: No.
P: No? *(reads)* 'wanted to eat them all'.
D: *(Pause, refers to book)* Meg took her caldron and made a spell.
     (T writes)
D: And Tyrannosaurus looked in the window . . . in the window . . . Stegosaurus and Diplodocus came in the door . . . *(impatiently)* and Stegosaurus and Diplodocus came in the door.

The parent again waits, prompts and queries. She invites the child to reflect upon his own text and the need to avoid repetition when she asks, 'We've already said that haven't we?' and asks him to consider, therefore, whether it needs saying again. However, there is no attempt to force the child away from having control over his own text. When the parent's later suggestion of looking for a 'reason' is rebuffed there is no issue made of it and the parent patiently continues to take down what the child is saying. However, the fact that such a thought was made explicit is a potential demonstration to the child of a need for things in the text to be there for a purpose. The rejection by the child may actually be a failure to understand the way in which the terminology is being used. The parent also offers a demonstration of fallibility; that adults don't know everything. She has to look in the book for the spelling of Stegosaurus. In both the above extracts the children are being offered insights into authorship which, although not taken up immediately, are becoming a consistent part of the experience of working with the parents.

In the third extract the parent is not only having to cope with two authors, but also one of the pre-school children who wants to get 'in on the act'.

P: Right girls, let's get our heads together 'cos this doesn't sound right at all and the little girl or boy . . . who is our book for?

E: Terry.

P: He isn't going to understand this at all is he? Listen *(she reads)* 'She telephoned her parents. Lucy's parents came to take her home. She was very happy to see them. Lucy was sad to leave Terry'. Ah . . . but she was sad to leave Terry . . .

N: Rub that bit out and . . .

P: She was very happy to see them but was also sad to leave Terry . . .
(E leaves the group and Steven, a two-year-old whom P is looking after, joins them. He has a felt tip pen and is casually mark-making at the bottom of the sheet on which P is writing)

P: 'And waved goodbye.' Anything else Nazia?

N: No it's finished.

P: Is it finished? No little bits? Aw! *(she spots Steven's activity)* Crime of crimes . . . you little horror bag.

N: *(Laughs)* Horror bag *(Steven moves his hand and he immediately moves his attention to another piece of paper with a picture on.)*

P: Don't write on that . . . look that's a beautiful picture that Esther's done.
(Steven again tries to write on P's draft.)

P: Right so what do you think, Nazia, have we finished or do we need to add a bit more . . . *(P uses her left arm to keep Steven at bay whilst keeping her attention upon Nazia)* . . . or do we need to add anything to the book?

S: *(Wriggling free)* No . . . no.

N: The book?

P: Yeh, do we need to add anything else?

N: Yeh.

P: What?

N: When Lucy got home she said 'when will I go again and at night time she couldn't sleep'.
(At this point Steven is experimenting with his pen, writing on his hand.)
So she telephoned up . . .

P: Don't you think if we did that, that would be part two to this book
      . . . part one?
      *(Steven has been watching P intently and realising she is absorbed in
      speaking to Nazia his hand slowly stretches over and he starts to write
      on her draft.)*

N: Yeh.

P: So do you think we could just finish part one and then remember
      that for part two . . .
      *(By this time Steven has moved right up to the paper and is busy using
      his pen.)*
      . . . because Lucy could go on for ever and ever and ever having all
      these adventures couldn't she *(looks at Steven)* . . . and Steven
      could keep on scribbling on my writing couldn't he? *(laughs)*
      *(P now attempts to pull back the paper. Steven pulls it back his way
      and even when she picks it up he still tries to get hold of it.)*

N: Naughty, naughty . . . naughty . . .

This transcript alone cannot do justice to the persistence of the younger
child in attempting to participate in the writing. The pre-school children
were frequently influenced by all the activity going on around them.
Their play area had been provided with pens and paper and there were
many writing-like marks lying around on the floor at the end of each
session. One child took his piece of paper and pen and actually worked
along side the children and parents.

   In the above transcript the parent presents the children with some of
the difficulties in their text. The parent is fairly persistent in her attempts
to invite the children to extend the text but here, it results in an addition
that looks rather like an excuse for a new story. The parent has to
backtrack and suggest that such an episode might have to belong to the
second part. Here the parent's intention to engender some kind of textual
revision has clearly failed, but at least the children are being presented
with a view that is not sycophantic while, at the same time, not one which
takes over control. It may be, as in the previous transcript, that the form
of the request is misunderstood by the child who interprets it in a
reasonable way, but clearly not in the way the parent intended. It is
characteristic of the children's interactions with the parents that they
were prepared to remain in control of their texts; they were not afraid of
refusing, or resisting ideas if they felt them to be inappropriate. This was
clearly part of what was, for the parents, a major learning experience
about young children in school.

   In the final extract we can see the parent being prepared to follow the
ways in which the children are sorting out their ideas. In the process, the
parent helps to legitimate the use, by authors, of books as sources of ideas
and knowledge.

N: *(Dictates)* She was a girl and she called Lucy.

P and E:*(Together)* The dinosaur's a girl called Lucy.

N: Yeh.

E: *(Dictates)* And her family lived on the moon . . .

P: *(Writes)* . . . and her family lived on the moon.

E: She came to America.

N: Shall I . . .

P: *(Writing)* . . . to America.

N: Shall I show this to the camera?

E: *(Dictates)* And she got here . . .

P: *(To N)* Yeh.

E: And she got to America by . . . because . . . she was a dinosaur with wings . . . she . . . she got here because she had wings.

P: *(Writes)* She came to America . . .

N: And she's all brown.

P: *(Writing)* . . . with her wings.

N: Shall I colour it in, yeah?

P: Yeh, what colour are dinosaurs?

N: Sometimes they could be brown.

P: Hmm.

N: When I've just coloured this in . . .

E: *(Producing a dinosaur reference book)* Dinosaurs.

P: Ah . . . now do you think she was happy in America without her family?

N: No.

P: Do you think she was a bit sad, maybe?

N: Yeh.

E: Can it be Tyrannosaurus rex?

N: Tyrannosaurus rex?

P: Well . . . do you think our Lucy . . . our Lucy is a Tyrannosaurus rex?

E: Now let's look in this book.

P: Go on then, we'll have a look and see if we can see Lucy.

E: Lucy isn't in there.

P: It's very hot where Lucy comes from isn't it?

E: She came from the moon.

P: Oh Lucy did, yeh, but real dinosaurs . . .

N: There's Lucy *(pointing to a picture)*.

P: Is that Lucy . . . is that Lucy when she was a little baby?

E: No it isn't.

P: Well perhaps it was Lucy when she was a little baby.

N: Yeh.

E: No.

N: And this is Lucy when she was big.

E: No that's Lucy when she was in her eggs.

P: Yeh, so if you look at that picture . . . that, Nazia, shows you before there's the eggs and that's Lucy the little baby, and do you know what that's called inside the egg? A foetus.

E: Right . . . that's Lucy when she was a baby and there's Lucy when she's just crept out of the egg.

P: Oh she's only a little baby there isn't she?

E: And let's see if we can find some of when she was grown up . . . if we can't we'll get another book.

P: Will we?

E: There's Lucy's footprints.

P: Yeh . . . what big feet . . . look at those footprints.
N: Yeh . . . and there she is . . .
E: No.
P: Oh no that's . . . do you think that's our Lucy . . . she looks all gruesome . . . she looks a bit vicious there.

The above episode starts with an interesting correction made jointly by the parent and one of the children. The correction is instantly accepted and the development of the story continues. As the text is being constructed the children realise that they need to have explanations to account for the dinosaur getting to America, so the dinosaur becomes a flying dinosaur. The parent introduces a reflective element with her question about whether the dinosaur is happy away from her family. The children follow their interest into the book and, in the way the parent handles this, the children's use of the book is legitimised. The whole episode is one which allows the two authors to deepen their understanding of an aspect of their subject.

In the four transcripts we can identify the partnership between the parents and the children. The authorship of the children is being facilitated and developed. This is not achieved by instruction or force, but by demonstration, question, and discussion.

The parents reflect

The effect of this experience upon the parents was extremely interesting and very satisfying. Although it had been many years since most of the parents had done any sustained writing, they were so delighted with their success that they elected to continue to meet as a writers' group. They have even produced a small booklet of their writing. In this, some of the parents reflect upon the shared writing with the children:

'Before doing this I thought all children were more or less the same according to their age, but I have since found out that they vary considerably. It is unbelievable to see how their minds work when they are desperate for more knowledge, and even harder to believe that they take everything in, but they do.'

'What I didn't consider was that the children I was involved with would have so many different ideas of their own and that I would find myself between two children trying to be better than one another in everything we came across in doing this book.'

'Lauren's tired, she wants some attention. Oh dear, we're never going to be finished. Miss Gregory is going to read her a book thank goodness. Quick, grab that pen. Ian's thought of a title and the first few lines of the story. There's even enough time for Ian to draw his first picture for the book. It's the end of this session and I'm starting to feel confident. I just wish it wasn't so hectic.'

Clearly this had been a distinct and valuable learning experience for the parents, as well as for the children.

Conclusion

It would be ridiculous to claim that as a result of this one project the children in my class had changed their views on authoring text. It was never envisaged that it would operate in such a direct manner. However, it is possible to make claims about the kind of experiences the children had which, if those experiences are reinforced, supported and extended, may well lead to changes in authorship. Working with the parents gave children confidence as authors. Here were adults who were prepared to take time to listen, to talk and support. At the end of the project each child had produced a very nice story and book, which was then passed on to the intended reader. The sense of success and achievement is absolutely vital in encouraging children to sustain interest in writing. In the course of their working with parents, the children were also exposed to alternative views about how people produce stories. The children were introduced to the importance of bearing the audience in mind, and re-reading the text to ensure coherence and to avoid repetition. They were helped to think about the interest of their stories and the construction of their texts.

In all the interactions the children were willing contributors; they were not cowed or repressed; they were constructing their own texts. They would listen to what the parents had to say, would respond, and sometimes act on the advice but, in the end were going to make their own minds up about what they wanted to author.

This chapter originates from work carried out during the development phase of the SCDC National Writing Project 1986–88 © SCDC Publications 1988.

— 10 — Authors review authors
Susan Williams

My classroom is a writing-rich environment. Within this environment the children have developed an interest in writing, are keen to write, and write frequently. A variety of writing experiences are provided within the classroom, with an almost total emphasis on helping the children develop as generators and communicators of meanings, in other words, as authors. The children have created books and poems, written letters and messages, kept diaries and journals, and have created newspapers.

The publishing and sharing of what is written plays an important role in helping the children develop understandings about authorship. The products of their authoring are mostly public. There are notice-boards and other display areas in the classroom for children to display, and refer to, messages, reminders, questions, notifications, and newly made books and poems. All their books have a place in the book corner and are shared regularly with other children.

As authors, the children have enjoyed creating a variety of books. At various times these have been initiated by both the children and myself but usually, the ideas for their books come from their own interests, each other, or from books written by professional authors. The children have a wide selection of literature in their book corner and their own books are displayed alongside the books written by professional authors. I try not to discriminate between printed books and the children's own books when reading and discussing what we have in our book corner. As a consequence the children's views about what constitutes a worthwhile book derive from discussions about many different types of books.

One of my major concerns is always to help the children reflect both on the writing process and the product which results. In an effort to facilitate this reflection, I decided to use the children's skills as authors to reflect upon the products of other authors. In other words, I wanted to see how my children could cope with becoming book reviewers. Book reviewing is a kind of metalinguistic task. It focuses on how an author has created certain kinds of experiences and meanings with words. I was hoping that by extending my children's experiences of reviewing I would be able to help them reflect upon their own authoring processes. The children had recently written one book review and those had been put on a special notice-board. These indicated little reflection about the books that had been read and were little more than single comments.

What is a review?

For the purposes of this chapter I am concentrating on the work of four five-year-old children of differing ability. It was important for me to establish early on what they believed a review was and I talked generally with them about book reviews.

Teacher: What is a book review?
M: . . . get a book and card and write all the words down and make a book.
Teacher: You write all the words down and make a book?
M: Yes, I mean, no . . . read a book and put the title on . . . do the picture.
Teacher: Is there a difference between writing a book review and making a book then?
M: They go in different places . . . reviews got felt tip round *(referring to the layout of the book review display board)* . . . they don't have them *(referring to books)*.

The child was clearly concerned with the physical manifestations, particularly those relating to where books and book reviews were displayed. The simple comment type reviews that the children had already written had been done on different paper from that used for the writing of stories. Clearly this had served to define for children some of the characteristics of a review and a story. Some children were able to offer a more conventional idea of a review.

RR: You can put the name of the book and put what it is about. Then they can find it and read it.
Teacher: Who can find it and read it?
RR: The children . . . you can write messages how you think books are.

J: The writing of a book
Teacher: The writing of a book?
J: The writing that you read about a book . . . what it's about.

As the discussion progressed so certain ideas became clearer:

RR: One's on card and one's on paper the . . .
J: A book review is different because book review is writing.
Teacher: A book review is writing?
J: Like in a book.
Teacher: How is it different?
J: You make a book review but books sometimes are made.
RR: Books are different.
Teacher: They're different?

RR:	Because they've got different pictures.
Teacher:	Is that the only difference?
RR:	No there's lots of stories and then you read them *(points to the book reviews)* and then you know how to read them *(points to the books)*.
Teacher:	So are they copying books?
RR:	Only the name.

Clearly RR was trying to inform me that she knew something about book reviews beyond their physical manifestations. She recognised that there had to be a content which offered some kind of comment about the reading value of a book. Further discussion indicated that there were other insights available.

M:	People make books so you can read them.
Teacher:	What about book reviews?
M:	So children can read them so children can read the book.
Teacher:	Children read them so they can read the book? Why do you read book reviews?
M:	Helps you read the book.
Teacher:	How?
M:	When you read it.
Teacher:	What does it say then?
M:	It tells you how it ends and in the middle what it's about.

RE:	You can pin books and book reviews up so that people will look at them.
Teacher:	So they read the book reviews?
RE:	To help them read books . . .
J:	It tells you what's in the book.
RE:	It tells you how it begins.
J:	It tells you how it ends and in the middle what it's about.
RE:	You can find out if it's a bit hard for you.

It was also clear that one or two of the children understood that there could be consequences after reading a book review.

Teacher:	What would you do next?
J:	I would read it and look at the pictures.
Teacher:	What if the book review said it wasn't very good?
J:	I wouldn't read it . . . go and read the others.
Teacher:	What about you? What if the book review wasn't very good?
J:	I'd see if I liked it.
RE:	If you see something that's very interesting you can go to the library . . . and buy them.

Clearly, although the children had only written review-type comments once before, several of these almost six-year-olds understood, to some extent, that a review commented upon a book and offered the reader a message about the worth of a book.

Following my initial discussions I asked the children to offer ideas about the kinds of things that should go into book reviews. Their ideas managed to cover a number of important features:

The story content

The layout or form i.e. were there chapters or individual stories in a book?

An opinion as to whether the book was worth reading.

An observation of something the children liked about the book.

First reviews

The children then chose some of their favourite books for their first reviews. The important factor when writing their reviews was not presentation, but composing something worthwhile about the book they were reviewing (see Examples 1, 2, 3, and 4).

Make a face

There are four stories in the book and it was a funny book. I like the stories they all fell into a pile. The pictures are funny.

Example 1

Molly move out

It has three chapters. It is horrible at the front. It is nice at the end and I like the pictures. They are lovely. It's about a rabbit.

Example 2

Jump frog jump

This is a book that rhymes and I like it very much and it's bad and good. I like it when the boy lets the frog out. Will you read this book?

JUMPY FROGG JUMP8

this is a Book that rhymes and I Like it veRY much and its BAd and good I Like it when the Boy Les the FRoc aUtwiLL you Read this Book

Example 3

Dear Teddy Robinson

It has eight stories in this book. It's about a toy shop and keeps house has a concert party and goes to the doll's hospital and meets a gnome and goes up a tree and he's a polar bear. All of the stories were good. But one of the stories were sad.

Dear   Teddy   RoBinJon   it   has
8   storys   in   this   Book   ies
aBoqt   a
havoSe   hds   toy   shop   and   keePs
goas   to   the   a   consat   Party
mits   a   chandolls   hgpitaL   and
a   tree   and   his   grom   and   up
all   or   the   a   poid and   gose
one   of   the   storys   were   Bere
storys   was   sad   good   8at

Example 4

There is nothing special about these pieces of writing; they are neither particularly good nor particularly bad. However, they do reveal young authors attempting to cast their views about a book into written form. All of the children believed that their opinions of the books were important – and indeed they were. The displayed reviews were read eagerly by the other children and tempted others to read the books being reviewed. However, the children found as they wrote more reviews, that it was necessary to use adjectives which were more precise than 'good' or 'nice' when they were describing the books. They started to think about the mood or type of story and extended their descriptions to include words like funny, bad, horrible or sad.

In general, the children found it very difficult to describe the plot of the stories. They tended to become engrossed in a description of a small part of the story, leaving the reader of the book review with limited insight into what the story was about.

Becoming more critical

In a relatively short space of time the children were becoming much more confident in their reviewing and some started to review books which they had not particularly enjoyed.

Michaella reviewed *Fearsome Fritz* by Jean Willis

'It was good, bad and scary. When it's good it's when the boy scares the parents. When it's bad it's when the men get the little boy. Fearsome Fritz is a bit naughty really. It's worth reading. Some of the pictures are very good and some of them are a bit scary. It rhymes a lot.'

Rebecca E reviewed *I can squeak*, one of the Ginn Rythym and rhyme books

'I didn't like this book because it has got different animals that I don't like in it. Other people can read it, they might like it. Some people might think it's good but I don't like it because they've got animal noises. They're horrible and most of the animal pictures.'

Rebecca R reviewed *Goodnight Owl* by Pat Hutchins

'The owl is the character in most of the story. I don't like this book because the animals wake the owl up. I like the pictures but the characters are nasty because it wakes the owl up. I just like one character the owl.'

Jodine reviewed *Peace at Last* by Jill Murphy

'I don't like this book. It's horrible and nasty at the beginning because daddy bear doesn't get any sleep. The pictures are horrible because daddy bear can't get any sleep and the words are too big for me.'

The children were, of course, also composing positive reviews of books they did like.

As the amount of reviewing grew, so did the skill in composing a review. This was apparent not only in their analysis of the book, but also in the way they began to incorporate words like 'character', and in the way their descriptions became more vivid. The children also began to offer explanations. The word 'because' was becoming a consistent feature of the reviews. They were also prepared to concede that other people may think differently about the book from themselves, as in Rebecca's comment that 'they might like it'; a clear recognition of the personal nature of reviews. Descriptions of the plot were also improving and references to presentation and readability were beginning to appear. For Jodine, the issue of whether the book could be read independently was beginning to become important.

Reviewing one's own work

Although many children in the class were writing quite a lot of reviews, they did not stop engaging in the composition of other kinds of texts, particularly stories. I wondered whether the children would be able to bring their reviewing skills to the examination of their own stories. I had always hoped that the process of reviewing would, in the end, make them more reflective about their own texts and here was a chance to see the extent to which children were able to evaluate these stories. The stories were ones which were completed and had already been put into the book corner. Unfortunately, there is not space here to present the stories but, nevertheless, the reviews make interesting reading:

Michaella reviewed her own re-telling of *Little Red Riding Hood*

Little Red Ridind Hood

its a veRY lovelY Book because I Presented the pictures and the writing good and Somn of the characters Were good and Somn of the characters weYe wicked like the wolf and I Really like Little Red Riding Hood I Recommend People to read it I could have made it better with Speech bubbles out of his mouth saying rrrrr

Example 5

Jodine reviewed her own story 'A baby and a girl and a boy'

A baby and a girl and a boy

lts about a baby and a and a girl and a boy they go To There Friends hase and they go To work its worth reading Because the pictures was coloured in ni as my best characters was the Babby its a happy story I llkyd it when the little girls Friend said she could come to the house

Example 6

Rebecca E reviewed her
story 'The giraffe'

The   giraffe

its   wooth   Rebing   because   it   a   good
Book.   is   a   boot   giraffes   who   get   caught
in   traps   is   sad   I hav   covloured   the
pictures   in   neatly   and   I   like
the   charactels   ov the   baby   gifafte
I   cud   made   seum   speech bubbles   ov
the   giraffe   saying   HLP.   I   recomending
it.

Example 7

Rebecca R reviewed her
story 'My baby Michaella'

my   BaBy   mykala

its aBout   a   BaBy   in   chapter   one
she   cras   for   her   Bottel   and   in
chapter   tow   she   gose   to   the   shops
chapter   one   its   happy   Becaus   she   gets
her   Bottel   at   the   end   chater
two   its a Bit   scary   Becose   the
strarjer   tras   to   get   her   the
stranjer   is   a   horaBel   caricter

I   shub   of   pat   spich BuBBls   from
the   stanjers   mout   the   BaBy
is   a   nice   calrcter   wood   you
like   to   read   it?

Example 8

The children proved to be enthusiastic reviewers of their own books. They were clearly more effective when describing the plot but, at the same time, there was less attention to the presentation and readability. Could this be because readability was not a problem where their own work was concerned? The quality of the pictures was very important to them and featured strongly in their reviews and they began to offer more insight into the nature of the characters. Throughout the composition of these reviews the children frequently discussed with each other the things which needed to be included (hence the frequent mention of 'speech bubbles'). The children were writing more and were beginning to make explicit appeals to potential readers. At this stage in their authoring careers the children were never tempted to change any aspect of their original texts after they had written their analysis. However, I see this move into the critical examination of one's own text as a precursor of a level at which one will take on editing, so the ground work was being prepared. It seemed an appropriate time to formalise this knowledge.

Guidelines for reviewers

I decided to ask some of the children to write draft guidelines for reviewing. They set about this task enthusiastically and produced some important points (see Example 9).

Book review guideines
Say Somthing aBout the Piters

Say Something aBout the Writing

does it rhyme or iust a
Story?

Say Something aBout recomending
it
is it a good Story?
IS it a FuNNy Book?
is it Sad?
is it scery?
Say somthning aBout the carictus.

Example 9

These were presented to a meeting of the whole class and some additions were made (see Example 10).

hwe is init ?

put the name of the
        Book doWN.

hwe writiNe the Book ?

hwe Made the picters?

hwe PuBLIShd the Book ?

What is the Book aBout?

Example 10

The guidelines were pinned up in the writing corner and it was obvious that as children continued to write reviews they were using those guidelines to think about what they should write, and to check, once they had written, that nothing had been missed out.

Conclusion

Prior to the children's work on book reviews they had a commitment to authorship and were not afraid to express their likes and dislikes when selecting material to read. However, when confronted with the task of reviewing the work of professional authors, they seemed to have restricted notions of what to do. As their experience grew so their control over their authorship of reviews grew and they were ultimately able to use these skills to evaluate their own stories. It was evident that the children acquired a much deeper understanding of the process and function of reviewing. When they write reviews now they do so with reflection, and skill. Taking on a review means adopting a perspective on how to handle text; it means trying to understand what an author was hoping to do and trying to understand one's emotional and intellectual response to what that author has written. The children in my class have a lot more to learn about reviewing books, but I believe very strongly that the experiences they have had, and the advances they have made, indicate an ability to take a reflective stance towards both other people's and their own texts.

— 11 — A journey into authorship
Nancy Pearson

Introduction

The writing experience of too many children in school is a seemingly endless burden of story writing. I have always been concerned that my children should author much more than stories. The opportunity to introduce the children to a range of different aspects of authorship came when I was sent a copy of the Ahlbergs' book *The Jolly Postman*.

The Jolly Postman includes letters written to various fairy-tale characters. This book fascinates children not only with the letters to the characters, but also with the illustrations and rhymes which cleverly depict how the postman's adventures transpire as he visits each character. I was able to use the book as a focus for a delightful set of authoring experiences for my second-grade children (seven years) at Washington School, Moorehead, Minnesota.

We decided to create our own version of *The Jolly Postman* but using, as a base for the authoring, those tales with which our children were familiar and which offered the same rich range of opportunities as those used by the Ahlbergs. To help set a context for our activity it was important to immerse ourselves in fairy-tales. If we were going to be able to write in character then we needed to become even more familiar with these fascinating stories. Reading the stories thoroughly was part of the reading/writing relationship of our authoring experiences. We began our fairy-tale unit by sharing books the children had brought from their own book collections. Some of the books were new and shiny, rarely used, while others had been used for several generations. The books were to be added to our special collection. Each child showed his or her book of favourite fairy-tales to the class. As the tales were shared the children noticed that there were a number of different versions of each tale, and began looking at the similarities and differences. As the children learned about unfamiliar tales and read some of them, we began talking about common themes which occur in fairy tales. The class decided that there was often a 'good guy', usually a victim of the 'bad guy'. Rachel offered that there were the sad and the scary parts. Those were the bad parts, but there were also the happy endings which were the good parts.

Our version

The first visit the Jolly Postman makes is to the three bears with a letter of apology from Goldilocks. The class discussed what was included in an apology and determined that it needed to tell what was wrong and who made the error, as well as to tell how it could be made right with a promise never to do it again. Of the stories that we had read, *The Little Red Hen* offered a great opportunity to create a letter of apology.

For reasons that will become clear later (but were unknown at the time to my class) it was important to use a particular version of the story. Consequently I had to decide which version of *The Little Red Hen* to use.

Dear little Red Hen,
How are you? I am sorry I did not help. I could help you the next time. We could get together. And you can come to my birthday. I will give you my phone number. And you can give me your number. We'll play with my toys and have some cake. Can you for give me?

Love,

Dog

(Rachael W.)

Example 1

For example, in one version the Little Red Hen grinds wheat, and in another she grinds corn, while her finished product could be either bread or cake; also in the different versions there were different animals as her 'fair weather friends'. To help the children understand that tales can change through many tellings I played the children's game of 'gossip' (Chinese whispers) with my class. The game is played by having a child whisper a sentence to another child who in turn whispers it to another, and so on until the sentence has passed through the entire group. The children were amazed at how the sentence had completely changed by the time the last child repeated aloud what he or she had heard. These experiences helped the children understand that books did not represent the final word on anything. They began to perceive that authors made choices and rewrote stories however they wanted. For the children, it legitimised their own freedom to create or amend as they wished.

After re-reading the story the children volunteered to role-play the various animals and apologise to Little Red Hen for not helping her make the bread. Each child chose which animal they would like to be, and they composed a letter of apology to Little Red Hen. After they had written drafts of the letter they worked on them, revising and editing. They then wrote on stationery and had a go at folding and fitting the letter in the envelope. The children discussed where the address, return address and stamp should be and they had an enjoyable art activity designing their own postage stamps.

Rachel, Adam and Mindy were pleased with what they had written and were eager to share their letters with the class (see Examples 1, 2 and 3).

Wed. 2/10/

Dear Little Red Hen,
I'm sorry I didn't help you bake the bread. I'll help you any day. I think you are nice. I'll say "yes" to whatever you say.

Love,
Cat (=AdamLee)

Example 2

Dear Little Red Hen,
I'm sorry I didn't
help bake the
bread. Next time
I'll help bake
the bread and cut
the wheat and
make the flour
and I might
even get a
piece of bread.

Love, Duck (Mindy)

Example 3

Each child added their own name as there would be several letters from each animal. Rachel and the other children 'mailed' their letters and then asked me if the Little Red Hen would really write answers. I replied that I was certain that she would as soon as she had finished her work. It was with much anticipation that Rachel and her classmates dropped their letters into the red mailbox in our room.

Although my class did not know it, the letters were all delivered to another class in the school. These children were aged ten and were sworn to secrecy. Amazingly none of the older children ever revealed to any of the younger ones that they were responding as the characters. Their class teacher, Althea Worth, followed much the same procedure as I had done (hence also the necessity for a fixed version of each fairy-story). She introduced *The Jolly Postman* and then discussed the nature of a letter of apology. Her class each chose a letter to answer (and included many creative illustrations). The letters were placed into envelopes addressed to the animal which had written the original apology.

There was great excitement when the letters were delivered. Letters were read aloud to the class and shared frequently between smaller groups of children. The older children had taken great pains with their replies. The reply to Rachel's letter read:

> Dear Dog
> I accept your apology. I will come to your birthday. I'd appreciate it if you could do some dishes for me. Do you have anything to do on Saturday? If you don't, you can plant some more wheat for me. Then we might bake another bread. What kind of cake do you like? I will get you a birthday present if I can. I can come and play with your toys. I can bring my baseball over if I can find it. Do you have any baseball cards? I will bring my basketball over. We will play a little 'one-on-one'. I will give you a ten point lead. When you said, 'How are you?', I am fine. I forgive you. Do you want Cat and Mouse to come over and play with your toys too? Well, Have to go.
> Bye
> Little Red Hen

Rachel was pleased with the personal touches in her reply and did not comment on the obvious athletic ability of the Little Red Hen.

In the Ahlbergs' story the Jolly Postman's second stop is at the home of the Wicked Witch where he delivers a circular showing all types of products that a witch might be tempted to buy. For our class letter exchange we chose to use the troll in *The Three Little Billy Goats Gruff*, and we listened to a story record that had imaginative sound effects to help us learn more about the possible characteristics of the troll. The children found several beautifully illustrated books of the story and, most excitingly, managed to borrow a large statue of a troll from another teacher.

To help the children understand the characteristics of a troll I decided to do a webbing activity with them on the blackboard, and then we discussed what kind of products might appeal to such a creature who lived under a bridge and scared goats. Next the children wrote rough drafts of their advertisements and we shared them in small groups in order to get input as to whether or not the advertisement would entice the troll to buy the products. The children soon learned that if they did not include certain basic information, such as the cost of the items, and where to send the order, the advertisement would be worthless. The final drafts were completed with colour and persuasive phrases such as 'all trolls love this'.

Rachel called her sales company 'Wackoo Bubble Gum Trick' and she offered the troll such items as:

> Chewed up bubble gum for five cents (The gum is done – give it to anyone)
>
> A lizard for twelve dollars
>
> An itchy shirt full of bugs for twenty dollars
>
> Bags of dirt and grass for a cent each

Rachel's terms were 'money or toys' with the promise that her products were guaranteed to work or 'your toys back'. Rachel's advertisement offered her the chance to play with language in an entirely different way from that of the letters of apology. There was a sense of great fun as the children vied with each other to invent unusual items and to find appropriate ways of describing those items. In a few days Rachel received this reply to her advertisement:

> Dear Rachel
> Hi! How was the grass? I would like to buy a lizard. I have enclosed a troll doll that is worth $5.50 and then some $7.50 (keep the change). I would also like some grass and dirt. I would like four bags full. I will send a beach ball that is worth 10 cents (keep the change). I think that will be it for now. Next time I will order more.
> Your friend
> Troll

The troll enclosed some carefully designed troll money and a self-portrait for Rachel to treasure. The troll money was thoroughly examined by Rachel and she would have liked to have gone immediately into the business of sales.

The third phase of the writing project was based on the Jolly Postman's delivery of a postcard from Jack (in *Jack and the Beanstalk*) to the Giant. In order to acquaint the children with postcard writing, they examined picture postcards and discussed the circumstances under which a person might send this type of written communication.

To give the class practice in identifying the main ideas that could be used to describe a holiday journey, the story of *The Gingerbread Man* was used. The children made accordion books with each page used to describe part of the journey. For the writing focus in this phase, we chose *Journey Cake Ho* by Ruth Sawyer, which is the story of a little boy who has to leave home because there is not enough food for him. In the course of his journey his cake falls out of his bag and rolls away. Needless to say, eventually all problems are resolved and there is a happy ending.

Each child designed the picture side of the postcard and then wrote their revised note and the address on the other side (see Examples 4 and 5).

I have been
on a Journey.
It was not fun
at all because
animals chased
me. I hope to
see you soon.
Goodbye
Love Johny.
Jasin

TO Merry
other side
TiPToP M
56560

Example 4

2/25/88

Dear Merry,
I miss you very much
I had a long journey
I passed many things.
The Journey cake
fell out of the bag I was very
scared.
         Love, Johnny (Dawn)

to Merry
Other side
TipTop Mount
    U.S.A.

Example 5

Rachel addressed her card to 'Merry, Other Side, Tip Top Mountain, USA', and wrote this message:

Dear Merry
I was sad when I had to leave but that was life. Then the
string broke. And my journeycake fell off and I chased it and I
went past a field full of cows and the journeycake said,
'Catch me and eat me as I roll by'. And then I passed a pond of
ducks. The ducks, a pig, some hens and a donkey all followed
me. I was scared! I miss you.
Love Johny (Rachel)

Rachel's short but informative text was again very different in style from the two previous texts. Both Rachel and the other children were revealing an ability to handle different genres in entirely appropriate ways. The children might lack experience, but they did not lack a sensitivity to the demands of the make-believe context.

Merry's answer to Rachel also came in the form of a postcard with a beautifully illustrated picture of Disneyworld. It seems that while Johny was off chasing his cake so Merry was away in Florida on a vacation. 'Merry' wrote:

We went to Florida. It was pretty neat. We went to
Disneyworld there. It was fun. We met Mickey Mouse,
Donald Duck, Minnie Mouse and Goofy. They were funny.
We had a little carnival, a dancing carnival. We joined in. It
was fun.
Love Merry

The Jolly Postman's next stop is to the home of Cinderella and her new husband, Prince Charming. Here he delivers a letter from a publisher who encloses a biographical book of Cinderella's life for her approval. For our writing exchange we used the story of *The Frog Prince* as the basis of a re-telling experience. The children really enjoyed telling their own versions and there was a great deal of variety in what they chose to do. Most of them used the same title but changed the plot by switching characters or the setting. One child made the heroine a frog who had been turned into a princess by a wicked witch, only to be released by the kiss of a handsome prince who was understandably very surprised to end up with a frog!

Rachel chose to follow the traditional plot of the story fairly closely, with her own sound effects added. Her draft read:

The Frog Prince

Ones upon a time their was a beautiful princes as beautiful as the sunset and a golden ball that looked like the sun. She was playing by a well and it fell in the well. Then a frog apeard and said, If I get your ball what will you give me? The princes said, my crown, thrown, food, jolrey, close? No no no no no I want to sit with you and eat with you a drink with yor from the same cup and walk with you and sleep in your nice silky bed and that is what I want. Will you give me all that if I get your ball? Yes I will. Promise. Promise. OK. He went down and came up. She grabed her ball and ran to her casle. The frog said, wait for me. But you promised. She put her ball in her bedroom and went to dinner. Well she was eating
she head this sond flip flap, flip flap, and a knock knock. She went to the door and she looked on the grownd and saw a frog and shut the door and went to the dinner table. Her father said, Who was that at the door? I will icksplane. So I think you should keep your promise. Knock knock. She let the frog in. He sat with the princes and he ate with her and he drinked with her and he sleped with her. She caryed him to her room and thowr him at the wall. Pooooooooph. The prince the princes screamed. The prince said, 'A wicked witch turned me into a frog. Now the spell is broken! And they got married.

Rachel's book was fairly small in size with an illustration on each of its sixteen pages. She chose soft colours for her illustrations, and she used 'balloon quotes' for some of the characters' speech. The cover showed the name of the book and a small uncoloured drawing of a frog, which was exactly as Rachel wanted it.

The answer from the publisher came in the form of a letter from Melissa of Storyland Publishing Company. Melissa wrote:

Dear Rachel
I like your story but on page 9 you spelled 'he' instead of 'her'. Why did the princess throw the frog to the wall? I also think you should write neater and make your picture neater. I forgot to tell you that you should colour on the cover.
Sincerely
Melissa

Although Rachel's reviewer was somewhat uncompromising in her reply, some of the children received rave notices from their reviewers. They were commended for their neatness, for their originality, for their correct spelling of words, and their illustrations. The 'Cool Kid Publisher' said of Chris' book that it was 'the best he had seen for years', and offered to publish it for five dollars. Although my colleague and I did not always agree with what our students wrote, we had decided that we would allow them to express their opinions in whatever way they wished so long as they were not cruel and always found something positive to say about the younger student's writings.

The next delivery by the Jolly Postman is a legal letter to the wolf from a law firm representing the three little pigs and Red Riding Hood. It accuses the wolf of harassment as well as wearing grandmother's clothes. For our exchange, we chose the story of *Rapunzel* because there is an interesting twist to the good guy/bad guy theme. To understand the plot of the story and to evoke feelings of empathy for Rapunzel and her parents, we made puppets of the characters. The children, in small groups, told the story using their puppets. By the time the children were ready to start to write their legal letters to the Witch they were using formal terms like 'kidnapping', 'child abuse', 'harassment', and 'abandonment'. All the children felt that the Witch was certainly deserving of the most drastic punishment, as Rachel and Dawn indicated in their letters (see Examples 6 and 7). When one considers the almost total lack of experience in writing formal letters of complaint or anger, then the performance of these children is remarkable.

Noty Law Firm

Dear Witch,
This letter is to inform you that giving rampeyen to aother people is allowed but taking a baby and we she is older you put her in a tower with no door and you clime up heir. well that is not allowed. And poor Hansele and Gretle. You were going to eat them. I thing I should put you in jail. But I am going to give you one more chance.

Sunsearly
Rachael W.
Lorre

Example 6

Renee Law Firm

Dear Witch,

This letter is to inform
you that you abused Rapunzel
when you cut her hair.
If you don't apologize
to Rapunzel you will get to
pay a fine of $60,000,00. And
for what you did to the Prince
there will be an extra of
$60,000,000.
So, beware.

Sincerely,
Dawn S.
Lawyer   *Example 7*

The Witch's answer to Rachel's accusation came in a letter from Susie, the 'Witch's lawyer from Yellow Law Firm'. This legal letter stated:

> Dear Rachel W
> I received your letter and I disagree. The Witch did not give rampion to the husband; he stole it. He promised to give up the child and you should keep a promise. The Prince climbed up the hair. Why shouldn't he be sent to jail, too? You know that would break Rapunzel's heart so don't send the Witch to jail.

As the class read their letters from the Witch's lawyers they began to appreciate that life is not always black and white; there are many grey areas. Not one of the children had realised that Rapunzel's parents were the cause of the problem, and they had to agree that keeping a promise is important, even when one deals with a witch!

Since the last letter delivery the Jolly Postman makes is to Goldilocks with a birthday card to open at her birthday party, our last letter exchange involved a party and some invitations. For this project we chose the story of *King Midas And The Golden Touch*. The lesson of greediness is one which the children could understand easily and the very thought of a father turning his own child, Marygold, into a gold statue because he wanted even more gold brought forth a very lively discussion. Rachel assured us that even if her mother won a million dollars on a sweepstake, her mother would give most of the money to the hungry and the homeless, because money given to you that you did not earn would only bring unhappiness.

Knowing that the story of King Midas had a happy ending was just cause for the children to invite Marygold to a celebration. We talked about the different types of invitations that a person might receive, and we considered situations where a person might need to reply to a formal invitation. Using the idea of an RSVP, the children each designed an invitation to Marygold and included a self-addressed reply card (see Example 8).

Time/Date - Thurs. 3/31/88 2:30 PM
Place - Room 168
  Telephone - 233-5259
No gifts necessary

R.S.V.P.   IT'S A BATCHELER PARTY !

Example 8

When Althea's children received the invitations all they had to do was to put a check (a tick) by the sentence stating '———I will come to the party' or '———I will not be coming to the party' and '———I will be bringing a guest' (see Example 9). The last option was necessary because Althea's class was larger, and my class needed to know how many guests to expect, even though they did not know the identity of the guests!

— I will come to th Party.
— I will not be coming.
— I will be bring a guest.   from Rachael
What kind of party?
A Welcome Back
Time 2:30 p.m. Date Thurs. 3/31/88
Place Room 168
Telephone 236-6400 no gift
from Rachael Winternes essy

Example 9

When the RSVP cards were returned, my class wondered if they were actually going to have a party. I assured them we were, and we began our plans. In the *King Midas And The Golden Touch* version that we used, the King and Marygold had a breakfast celebration. We decided to duplicate the menu as far as possible. We had grape juice to drink and our sausages took the form of sausage on a bun. The class made place mats for themselves and their mystery guests, and they prepared their versions of the Jolly Postman's letters to share. These books contained a personally illustrated page for each of the six fairy-tales we used, and a page with a pocket for their letters and the replies they had received. The class had composed a shared writing poem about our writing journey and each child's book contained the verses which functioned as a linking and explanatory rhyme.

All was ready for the party, when a knock was heard on our classroom door. There was a great deal of apprehension because the children didn't know who was going to come to the party. As Althea and her class came into our room my children were very shy and uncomfortable. The climate of the room soon changed as the older students identified with the particular letters they had written, and began examining the children's books. By the time the food was served both classes were delighted to have met their fairy-tale penpals.

Conclusion

During our letter exchange my children had continually surprised me by their ability to slot into the character from whose stance they were writing. They also surprised me by the way they were able to take on the demands of being different kinds of authors. They were able to be apologetic; they were able to be formal and angry; they were able to re-tell, in literacy style, a story; they could plan and organise a complex invitation, and they could adopt the more casual style of a postcard. They certainly have a great deal more to learn about these, and other, forms in which people write but, nevertheless, their responses clearly showed that as authors they were beginning to be sensitive to both audience and context. Inevitably, the real test comes when the children make a voluntary decision to use what they have learned about different styles, to generate their own texts in contexts different from *The Jolly Postman*. However, our own Jolly Postman exchange had provided the children with an opportunity to explore authorship and it had provided me with a wonderful chance to learn just how competent my children were as authors.

— 12 — Collaborative authorship
Mary Greaves

As a teacher of young children (six- to seven-year-olds) it had always been my concern to develop writing through a variety of experiences, usually initiated by myself, which I presumed would, through practice, facilitate the development of written language skills. I gave the children what I believed was a suitable environment for fostering written language; they were able to work in groups, pairs, or alone, and they could always come and talk to me about their work. It was my belief that I was giving the children the opportunity to be written language users, and to develop their abilities in a variety of situations.

The children with whom I worked were competent with many formal written conventions, and appeared to show clear understanding when faced with some kind of structured composition. However, as I observed the children it became clear that many of them did not show the same ability, and were often reluctant to write even when given the freedom to write in any way they wished. Why should this be so? I wondered if the reason was that the 'structured' composition allowed the children the chance to go on repeating acquired skills in a predictable way, whereas 'free' composition presented a threat in that it made demands upon them over and above the formal, conventional ones.

When I examined what the children were expected to do in 'free' composition, I began to appreciate that it was not quite what I had imagined it to be. Taken at face value, 'free' composition would suggest a situation where children have control over, and freedom with, their texts. However, it had become apparent that this was far from the case. The overall evaluator and assessor of both 'free' and 'safe' writing was the same — myself. Therefore, in both cases the children were intent on satisfying what they perceived as my fundamental requirements, and to them it seemed as if the requirements were always the same. The problem for the children when engaging in 'free' writing was in trying to resolve the paradox of being free and yet having to meet certain kinds of conventional constraints imposed by myself. They resolved their dilemma by sticking with what they perceived to be my most important criteria. The result was 'safe', non-risk-taking writing. I had, through my demands for neatness and accuracy with conventional skills, prevented the children from taking responsibility for, and control of, their own texts.

Since my discovery of this constraint upon their writing I have been exploring opportunities for increasing the children's awareness of their own texts. This has resulted in a shift away from more structured, controlled composition, to offering the children activities which allow them to function more validly as authors.

The following report is about one such experience that arose in my class. It has increased significance because I was able to record the entire sequence and as such, the data provides a rich resource for examining how the children functioned as authors during the complete development of a sustained piece of text.

The task

The situation arose when the reception class teacher in my school asked me if the children in my class would like to make some story books for her class library. She explained that it would be interesting for her class to have access to material written by known authors. I told my class that the children in the reception class were very interested in books and reading stories and had expressed a wish to read storybooks written by our class. Materials were provided and the children told that if they wished to participate, either alone, or with others, they could do so. Four of the children (David, Michael, Helen and Jackie) approached me, telling me that they were going to write a story for the younger children. At the same time they requested that they work together and have access to lots of books for ideas. We agreed that they could write in the infant library and the children selected the materials they wanted and took them to the library. It was anticipated that the children would work in the library for short periods of time during several days. In return for allowing them to do this, I asked them if they would allow me to record all their discussions while they were in the library. The children agreed.

I do not know whether it was because they really did not mind, or whether they thought they had no option but to agree. Either way it did not seem, from listening to the tape, that it made any difference to their behaviour. It was rare for any of them to refer to the tape-recorder, and it certainly did not prevent them from having disagreements or sometimes 'being silly'. The children took the recorder with them each day and set it up themselves. Throughout the sessions the children worked alone with no supervision; only occasionally did they return to the classroom to collect materials. The complete activity, including the rough draft, designing the book, and editing and writing it out, took place over three days, and involved five sessions of varying lengths. The total time spent on this task was one hour and forty-five minutes. The tapes were transcribed fully; a difficult task, but one which proved invaluable in discovering how these young children had set about the task of authorship.

Recording the children's discussions was a necessary part of my attempt to find out how my children performed as authors. The existence of an actual text is not, in itself, sufficient to allow good judgments about how children perform as authors. With young children, there may be quite a difference between what they know and what they can put on to paper. By recording the discussions I hoped to be able to find out how they saw the task, what kinds of demands they set themselves, how they met those demands, and what were critical components of their authorship.

Analysis of the transcripts revealed overwhelmingly that for these children, authorship was an interactive activity; it was a social event. Throughout, there was continual discussion, support, encouragement, opinion, critique, and analysis. The amount of 'talk about' far exceeded the actual time spent mark making. This offered time for reflection and composition. Also, books were continually referred to for ideas relating to content, spellings, illustrations and layout. This is not surprising; indeed it is a highly intelligent thing to do. When asked to create a storybook, what better source of demonstration is there than books themselves. It also revealed that the children recognised that the task imposed certain kinds of demands upon them which could be clarified by the examination of books and texts produced by published authors.

The early sessions

The first session was mostly spent on what might be termed organisation and 'starting off'; that is dialogue which helped the children form working groups, select topics, and discuss the perceived task and its audience.

The overall organisation of the children themselves was sorted out early on:

D: So we all do a big story together?
H: You two can do it together and us two can do it together.

However, the selection of a topic to write about was a slower process, and one which involved considerable discussion and negotiation:

J: I'm doing an adventure one.
H: In the woods . . . lots of trees and it's about a boy.
J: What?
H: It's about a boy and he's very naughty and when they're putting wallpaper up he wants his name putting on the wallpaper and he paints on the wallpaper and next day he does, and he looks in his mum's bag – gets her purse and chucks it down the toilet and flushed the chain.
J: You can't do that!
H: Right what are we doing?
J: What about Jack and the beanstalk or something like it?
H: I'm doing in the woods, a discovery.

D: I don't know what to do. What will we do, Michael?
H: I'm going to do something about school. Not this kind of school. I'm going to do something about a boarding school. It's one of my books at home about a girl called Isabel.
D: What can we do the story about Michael?
M: I know, Danger Mouse.

The children ranged through many ideas, often influenced by the books which surrounded them. The problem was not simply to find a good subject, but to find a good one which they could agree about. In the above extracts 'H' has some extended vision of what possibilities exist whereas the others are much more inclined to think in general terms about a topic.

Within their pairs the children negotiate their responsibilities:

D: Michael do you want to write it down and I'll tell you it?
M: No.
D: Go on then we'll do a bit each, you start.
M: One night . . .
D: One night he looked in the sky and he said . . .
M: He said . . . I'll give the moon a birthday present.
D: We'll write a sentence each.
M: One.
D: No, that's not a sentence that's a word.
H: He's copying that!
D: No we're just doing that because we don't know how to start.

They also demonstrated a certain kind of flexibility, although unfortunately in the following instance their perceived demand for accuracy led to a less interesting text:

D: Can I do a sentence?
M: And the moon said would you like to come to my party . . . birthday party . . . oh no, I've done two Ts.
D: Rub it out.
M: Right
D: And he replied – I'll look for that word in this book . . . its not in. Do you know how to spell 'replied' Jackie?
J: No.
D: Michael instead of replied shall we do 'said to'.

The discussion that took place had an important role in defining the nature of the task and, indeed, in keeping the children on task. Comments like 'you can't copy off books', 'it's quite good that', 'I can certainly get something from that one', 'you make the story up yourself and you put what it's called', 'what are we going to do about it?', 'we do it on this paper, we write the title on the top, don't we?', 'it's all right getting the title but you can't copy the story out of the books', 'you're supposed to make it up', all helped the children stay focused on the activity and demonstrated clearly that they were monitoring not only their own efforts but those of the others in the group.

The comments sometimes forced the other person to readjust, modify, or justify their judgments:

M: We'll do about the bear and the moon inviting him to a party.
H: The moon invited the bear to a party?
M: Yes it's a talking moon this one.

And sometimes ensured that the audience for which the stories were intended was not forgotten:

D: I know, I'll write this for my brother . . . it's for a boy this.
M: No, we've got to think of a story for everyone.

That the emphasis of the talk during the first session was on organisation and ideas was an important indication of the children's ability to respond as authors. The children knew that they had an extended period of time and knew that they did not have to put down the first thing that came into their heads. They also knew that there was an audience who would want to read their books. The talk shows young children making a great number of decisions about many aspects of the creation of a text; not just how to spell and write it neatly.

   The second and third session saw the children focusing more tightly on the content of the stories. Any authoring activity entails many thought processes before attention can be given to the final presentation. The interaction which took place allowed children to explore their developing text. The children, in developing their stories, constantly analysed, and were critical of, their work. They questioned, disagreed, debated and made decisions about how to proceed which demanded the editing, correction and re-drafting of the text. The following two extracts provide an opportunity to see what I would consider to be fairly typical dialogue relating to the content of the story:

M: One night a bear looked up at the moon and the moon said to the bear 'would you like to come to my party'.
D: And the bear said 'yes I would like to come to the party' . . . (*Michael writes*) . . . and the bear said yes I would like to come.
M: No, 'yes please'.
D: 'Yes please' said the bear.
M: 'Yes thank you'.
D: No shall we do 'yes I would like to come to your party indeed'.
M: That's good.

D: . . . but one alien jumped so high it landed on the bear and squashed the moon's birthday present.
M: No I don't want to do that.
D: And the bear started crying.
M: After that the bear went home.
D: Yes, no, and squashed the moon's birthday present.
M: No and it hurt the bear so much the bear started crying and went home.
D: Yes.

There is a clear exchange of views, each given expression, consideration and either rejection or acceptance and, often, followed by further debate. The debate follows a reasonable and detailed sequence, frequently concentrating on the choice of a single idea or word. By having the opportunity to develop these strategies, the children were not only able to express their own ideas, but to experience the views and strategies of others. Such interactions were helpful in that they encouraged the development of individuality, creativity and the ability to reason. Such reasoning helped the children to focus upon a central feature of authorship; that the choice of words does make a difference. The children in this group were able to work in a collaborative way and share their views. The level of debate was high and at no time did it develop into an unresolved problem, in fact after reaching agreement, the initially opposed party often acknowledged the result with a compliment.

The children demonstrated one other important feature of authorship; the recognition that they needed to keep reading what they had written. References to reading back were common:

'I'm just going to read through this. I don't know what to do.'

'Let's read it.'

Such re-reading offered the children the chance to maintain consistency and coherence, particularly when issues of some complexity had surfaced:

D: Just aliens.
M: How do you spell that?
D: A L I N E S.
M: Aliens jumping about.
D: The aliens jump-i-n-g.
M: About.
D: No, jumping and kicking about.
M: Jumping up and down.
D: Jumping up down yes.
M: D-o-w-n.
D: Jumping up and . . .
M: D-o-w-n.
D: Yes.
M: Let's read it now David?

Re-reading is also a pleasurable activity. One can take satisfaction in what one has written; it is, to some extent, a way of acknowledging one's success.

The later sessions

The fourth and fifth sessions were concerned more with the editing and presentation of the story in the form of a book. It could be argued that much of the activity in those sessions, in particular creating illustrations, is not directly related to the authoring process. I would disagree. The purpose of the activity was to produce a story 'book'. Throughout the sessions the children had used books as a source of reference for the content and organisation of their stories. Now they were able to do the same with respect to the design and illustration of their own stories. For many children writing is synonymous with drawing and is therefore, in their eyes, a valid and necessary part of the total authoring process. From my point of view I justify its inclusion in this chapter as a relevant aspect of storywriting; for without analysis of this aspect I would be failing to

view the development of the activity as a whole. From the children's
point of view its inclusion was a way of maintaining control over all
aspects of the presentation of their work. If it is in any way true that the
medium is part of the message, then the children were right to see control
over these aspects as part of the authoring process. Many published
authors would like such control over their work.

During the fourth session the children were mainly involved with
designing a book cover; this included an illustration and the title. Much
of the dialogue revolved around what was earlier referred to as
organisational action. In this case, it was the organisation in dealing with
the structure of the design. All the children chose to write the title in
capital letters, not an unusual choice considering that they are
surrounded by an environment which use this form quite extensively, but
perhaps of significance in that many teachers of young children still insist
on the use of lower case lettering to the exclusion of all else. The dialogue,
once again, showed rich interaction; questioning, defining and evaluating
the situation.

D: Shall we do this black?

H: Do a little picture of the bear.

M: Like that? (*referring to a library book*).

H: You should have asked if you could have done a design.

M: B-e-capital one.

D: Yes.

M: All capitals?

M: Put a little dot.

D: Birthday moon, you'd have dot, dot, dot, everywhere.

H: You have to have full stops.

M: What's your called?

H/J: Fishing on the river.

J: I do fishing . . . you do on . . . I do river.

D: We can colour ours in . . . do you know why we did ours like this?
       (*referring to the letters in the title*).

H: Well we're going to be able to colour ours in.

D: We'll just do this and this . . . then you'll be able to do your two
       won't you Michael...what colour shall I do them stripes, red?

M: Orange.

D: Yes orange.

M: I'll do the red . . . what colour shall we do the moon, David?

D: Yellow.

D: Michael so you're colouring all that bit, so I can colour the hat in.

M: What colour . . . blue?

D: Not blue . . . green.

M: If I do a whole lot of this, you can do the eyes and nose.

D: No, you do all that . . . do you know why because I write it all, didn't
       I? (*David wrote the title*).

M: Oh yes.

It is interesting to note at this point that even though the children had
different responsibilities, the children still maintained joint ownership of
their work, still used the plural 'we' to describe their actions, and were

always concerned with the equality of the workload.

In the fifth and final session the children made the pages for the book. Just prior to this session the children approached me asking if I would read their stories and check for any incorrect spellings. At my enquiry as to why the children wished me to do this, I was informed that while they considered their writing acceptable, their completed books would be presented for others to read and, as such, it was important that spellings were correct. They also added that because the children who were going to be the readers were younger, the experience of reading provided by the books should be in line with conventional, published story books. As Helen put it, 'When you buy books you don't find spelling mistakes in them'. The fact that I was approached and given the above reasons signals a significant level at which these children were functioning. Although there had been concern for spelling while they were drafting their stories, it was rare that concern for accurate spelling dominated the children; it therefore did not usually stop them thinking about the content. However, having completed their draft they revealed that they were sensitive to notions of correctness, and sensitive to the needs of their readers.

This awareness developed, I believe, not through the children being presented with a demand for accuracy but because they were functioning as authors who knew they had readers. All too often correctness in skills appears an end in itself when children are being taught to write. On the whole, there is little evidence from the transcripts of their specific regard for their audience but this conversation showed clearly that although it was not voiced, it was ever present in their view of the task which they had undertaken. It is a clear reminder that the absence of comments or specific evidence for a certain type, or level, of awareness should not be taken as evidence for inability or lack of knowledge.

Throughout the activity the children constantly referred to the books in the library where they worked. The last session was no exception. In one sense it indicated that the children saw a relationship between the activity they were undertaking, and that performed by 'real' authors. As authors it was important for the children to get it right, and what better model could they have. Books provided them with demonstrations of conventions used by published authors and these were debated frequently.

D: Get a book.
H: Copy the pages, you could do a picture.
J: Like this? *(referring to a library book)*.
D: I know what you mean.
H: Picture on one side, story on the other?
M: You can do it like that *(referring to library books)*.
D: Shall we do it like the first page?
H: I'll do a big picture and some writing underneath.
J: Could be the picture on one side, story on another?
M: Shall we do it like the first page underneath? *(referring to the writing)*.
M: Picture on one side.

D: Shall we do it like the first page?
H: Do a big picture and some little writing underneath.
J: Do some lines.

It is particularly noticeable on the tape of this session that there is a sense of 'nearing completion'. The whole process moved quickly in comparison with earlier sessions which, of course, included lengthy discussion about the content. A good deal of dialogue in this final session concerns the presentation of the composition, and includes talk about page references, punctuation and the aesthetics of the image of the work. There was also a sense of fun; something that is a most underrated aspect of learning to write.

The draft of the story
by Michael and David

one night a Bear looked up at the moon and the moon said to the Bear wulde you like to come to my party yes siad the Bear I would like to come to yore party siad the Bear so the next night the Bear set off to the moons party but when the Bear got ther ther was no other Bears ther ther were just alines jumping up and down but one aline jumped so high it landed on the Bear and it hert the Bear so much the poor Bear went home

Example 1

Having completed their storybooks the children were invited by the reception class teacher to read their stories to her children. Following the reading, the books were placed in the library with the appropriate tickets, showing the titles and naming the authors. The children's work was therefore given a kind of institutional legitimacy. Inevitably the successful experience of these children led to many other children producing stories for the library, either individually or, more commonly, collaboratively.

Conclusion

From my point of view this 'success' was achieved primarily by giving the children the opportunity to interact with each other during authoring experiences. Learning in isolation is infinitely more demanding than learning through cooperation and is much less fun. Interactions can provide both social support and social energy. There is evidence to show that with their peers, children are more likely to clarify or challenge ideas through questions, to offer suggestions, or to explain ideas to the less-informed. This type of interaction is often more complex than deliberately structured teacher-child talk. These children, in working together, often helped one another with topic selection, sustained one another as they wrote, offered advice about spelling, punctuation and organisation, volunteered suggestions for revision and, most importantly, were often an interested audience.

These children may not be 'good' authors in a conventional sense. Their stories have many faults. Nevertheless, the strategies they used to produce their books reveal authorship in action. They are bringing thought to bear on the marks they make and the ways in which they present those marks. The collaboration between the children allowed all of them to learn more, from each other about being authors. They will now look in different ways at texts produced by other authors and will undertake the generation of their own texts in a more reflective way.